WIRED

MUSICIANS' HOME STUDIOS

Tools & Techniques of the
Musical Mavericks

by Megan Perry

Backbeat
Books
San Francisco

Published by Backbeat Books
600 Harrison Street, San Francisco, CA 94107
www.backbeatbooks.com
email: books@musicplayer.com

An imprint of CMP Information
Publishers of Guitar Player, Bass Player, Keyboard, and EQ magazines

CMP
United Business Media

Distributed to the book trade in the US and Canada by
Publishers Group West, 1700 Fourth Street, Berkeley, CA 94710

Distributed to the music trade in the US and Canada by
Hal Leonard Publishing, P.O. Box 13819, Milwaukee, WI 53213

All interior photos are by the author.

Cover Design by Richard Leeds – BigWigDesign.com
Front Cover Photo by Jay Blakesberg
Text Design and Composition by Michael Cutter

Library of Congress Cataloging-in-Publication Data

Perry, Megan
  Wired : musicians' home studios : tools and techniques of the musical mavericks / by Megan Perry.
     p. cm.
  Includes index.
  ISBN 0-87930-794-3 (alk. paper)
  1. Sound studios—Equipment and supplies. 2. Sound—Recording and reproducing. 3. Musicians—Homes and haunts. I. Title.

  TK7881.4.P45 2004
  781.49—dc22
                                                2004009027

Printed in the United States of America

04 05 06 07 08   5 4 3 2 1

Contents

Dedication

To Bret Moore

Introduction

THE CONCEPT FOR *Wired: Musicians' Home Studios* has its roots in my own experimentation as a musician. Dabbling in piano, cello, and guitar, I found myself wondering how my favorite artists captured the sounds and wrote the songs that inspired me. This served as the catalyst for exploring the correlation between sound, science, and from-the-gut-technique exemplified by each of the subjects in this book.

While documenting the studio work of numerous artists for magazines like *Alternative Press* and *Rolling Stone*, I noticed that some of my favorite bands—Nine Inch Nails and Garbage in particular—did much of their work in their own home studios. Although neither of these bands became part of *Wired* (at least not in this edition), I soon found a host of other artists who are on the forefront of home recording.

From Snoop Dogg's home-style commune Tha Chuuch to BT's pristine studio enclave he shares with computers and digital drives, from Jonathan Davis's custom backyard bungalow to Daron Malakian's garaged-out home setup, musicians of all genres are making their own music their own way. This book aims not only to explain how these musicians compose and record their material but also presents gear lists, firsthand accounts, and more than 100 photos to illustrate how musicians at any level can use the same tools, tricks, and techniques as these musical mavericks.

Each chapter includes Tech Talk tips from the band, producers, and engineers that give a pro's view on how to create a recording space, build the right collection of gear, and—perhaps most important—learn the art of recording music. Many of these principles apply whether you are using a simple boombox or four-track to record your music, or are tracking through a top-of-the-line console or any of the more cost-efficient digital recording and editing systems described throughout *Wired*.

Whether you are soundproofing your basement for the first time or buying your first digital audio workstation, you'll find every aspect of your home studio is an important extension of yourself. Most studios reflect the personality of their owners, and environment is an integral part of instigating the creative process.

Perhaps just as interesting as the technical details and individual studio styles is the fact that as home-based recording techniques and equipment become within the reach of all practicing musicians, a new set of music-industry dynamics comes into play. More and more bands are trying the home-core recording approach for everything from simple demos to full-length albums. At the same time, record labels are beginning to adjust their business structures to stay in step with the rapidly changing retail landscape. What's the outcome of all this? We may see fewer artists in high-end recording studios and more home recording studios like the ones profiled here.

If the home studio trend continues, perhaps more important than *Wired*'s numerous gear lists and technical deep-dives are the discussions of the heart and soul of recording—and the role that producers and engineers like Michael Beinhorn and Frank Filipetti play in the process of shepherding a recording through the delicate balancing act of combining art, science, and commerce.

Musicians need a new set of skills in this paradigm, in which they must wear the hats of producer, artist, and engineer all at once. This renaissance spirit is alive in all of the artists profiled in *Wired* and is a staple of a new breed of musicians. Their most salient lesson is simple: It takes more than a good mic and a great mixing board to record great music.

But a vintage Neve doesn't hurt.

Chapter One

Michael Beinhorn
Venice Beach, California

"The whole business is falling into chaos. It's a shame really, because it promotes a devolution of the recording process."

PRODUCER MICHAEL BEINHORN'S NAME is frequently bandied about in the soundproofed walls of recording studios due to his purist opinions about analog. He has a track record of A-list clientele including Soundgarden, Hole, Herbie Hancock, Korn, and the Red Hot Chili Peppers, and his 20-plus-year career in the music business has given him the kind of clout that few share. His energies of late have been focused on something more than producing: He's maintaining his own self-sufficient semi-pro studio with an eye toward filling a gap he sees in the modern recording industry. As a producer—where the art of creating music collides with the grittier business side of making money from the trade—Michael has a lot to say about being inside the "belly of the beast," and gives his insight into understanding the dichotomy of his role. He has to mold creative products that are up to music-industry spec—one that can be hard to meet, since it involves packaging creative moments as a commodity. Michael discusses the role he sees for his studio, Standard Electrical Recorders, in the recording industry as well as how owning a studio has allowed him to experiment with (and warm up to) the science of digital recording.

First and foremost, Beinhorn is opinionated. He is an intelligent producer with a biting wit who knows the music industry inside and out. He speaks his mind, whether his sentiments are welcomed or not. That's his job: to listen and give bands his opinions—creative, musical, and otherwise.

Michael Beinhorn's Standard Electrical Recorders studio.

Michael begins with music-industry basics: control and money. "We producers are all control freaks," he says. "We all want to keep the money." Gentle, self-inflicted jabbing aside, there's a lot of truth to that. It is a producer's job to keep things in control, making sure they add a clear and concise vision to the project without going over budget. This is perhaps most important with bands that have creative differences. Musicians are often irritable and delicate creatures, and it is Michael's duty to listen with an unbiased ear and make creative decisions that complement the bands' sonic output without detracting from their musical vision. The purpose of this control is inexorably tied to money. Everyone likes money to some extent; life is just a bit easier if there are no worries about money. In the recording industry, the earning and distribution of money often comes under fire. Artists should get paid, producers should get paid, record executives should get paid, but all in accordance with how much music is selling as well as who is making the machine run. For most musicians, this means the creative people

Michael's "control room," from the outside looking in.

should get most of the pie. For the executives, this means the business should get most of the pie. Understanding both sides of the issue, Michael has a unique perspective on the recording industry's economic situation and its import for recording studios, including Michael's own Standard Electrical Recorders.

In the early 2000s, the music industry found itself in a huge nosedive. Some blame it on MP3 file-sharing, while others blame it on the poor quality of albums being released. Either way, when the music industry is not doing as well, the shakedown is felt everywhere, including at the recording studios. If the music industry is doing well, it tends to flood high-end recording studios with large-budget projects, and in turn the high-end studios turn a nice profit. But if the industry is experiencing a downturn, the labels lower their recording budgets. Many of the newly signed bands and even a few of the more established bands can no longer afford the higher-end studios. In turn, the same facilities that were charging $2,000-plus per day find themselves gagging for work. They often have to lower their daily rates and add incentives for clients to book time.

"Collecting gear is a bit of a sickness—no, it is a major disease. There is something very wrong with us producers, especially the ones who have been bitten by the gear-collecting bug. It is very unpleasant and depletes you of everything, unless you are making scads of money." —Michael Beinhorn

---

(Below) A line of guitars leads to the upstairs storage area. (Right) Racks of gear form a barrier between the live room and control room.

Due to what business insiders are calling a faltering state of the music industry, there is a new kind of studio subculture growing, where artists are in a way taking the music back into their own hands in the form of home studios and semi-professional studios. Some of the facilities being constructed are solely for the artists themselves, while others are privately owned with professional-quality recording gear, able to record full album projects without compromising sound quality. Michael Beinhorn's Standard Electrical Recorders is the latter. His semi-pro facility adds a new dimension to the recording world by filling in the gap for musicians who cannot afford the higher-end studios, or bands that are given a lower recording budget. Michael explains, "When I established this place three years ago, labels were handing out the money, so there were still large recording budg-

A Diezel guitar amp and a variety of effect pedals occupy space on the control room floor.

ets to be worked with—a band could spend three or four months in a studio without going over budget. Some major labels were still doing that as recently as six months ago, but that is long gone, and I don't see that returning anytime soon." Michael continues, "The whole business is falling into chaos. It's a shame really, because it promotes a devolution of the recording process. I still would much rather work at a professional studio, because it is a place with tons of high-quality gear, and the people working there know what they are doing—that is, generally speaking."

As the major labels continue to shrink recording budgets, Michael continues to ramp up his studio. Instead of using it only as a place to record guitars or vocal overdubs, he records entire albums at Standard, except for the drums. His small studio now fits a specific dynamic developing in the recording community. "I think there needs to be a middle ground between working in the nicest recording studios throughout the world and working in your bedroom. I hope this represents a nice middle ground. It's great to have an alter-

A rack of outboard gear includes a Neve stereo compressor, an ADR Vocal Stressor, a Moog filter, a few dbx 160 compressors, two UREI 1176 compressors, and a Summit mono tube compressor.

More of Michael's Wall of Sound: an Ampeg bass amp, a dbx compressor, and even more pedals.

native studio like this, because if I am not given a large budget, I can bring bands into my studio and save money. I have to be realistic now, and since budgets are getting tight—and they will definitely be getting tighter—it's important to be able to incorporate the budget factor with this studio." Summarizing the state of the recording studio within the industry's grim climate, Michael is realistic in his expectations: "You are not going to make money with this type of studio, even if it is uncomplicated and basic. You weren't going to make money having a small studio several years ago, and you sure aren't going to make money running one right now."

Regardless, Beinhorn is making Standard work for his own purposes. He can now bring in projects that may have lower budgets and still make the result musically innovative without sacrificing sound quality. This is a hot button for Michael, and he feels passionately that artists shouldn't have to sacrifice their unique sound, or the CD's overall sound, because of not having a large recording budget. Even though his studio is small, he wants to make sure what comes out of his space is top-notch material, both audio-wise and performance-wise.

Michael's ingenuity and his love for sound coloration has led him to set up his studio with top-quality gear while keeping his costs low. "You can take a space like this, and gear-wise make it comparable to just about any high-end studio. For instance, I have all of the microphone preamps that I could ever want for drums. Most of my preamps are Neve 1057s—they're very old, like the first series of the Class A transistor stuff—and 1052s." Michael's impressive gear collection lets him experiment and attain great sounds. "I am lucky that I have been able to acquire all this gear. It makes it easier to work at my place." His love for traditional recording methods can be seen within his arsenal of microphones. "I lean more toward Old School recording equipment, certainly on the microphone side. A lot of high-end

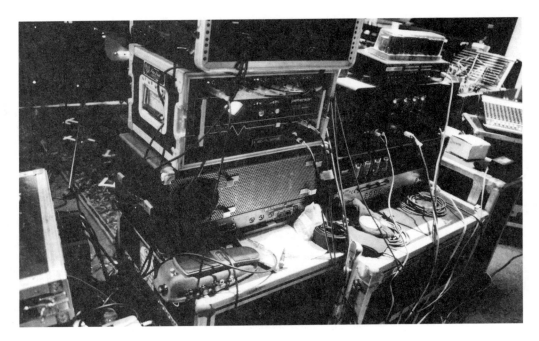

Tube amps and a Peterson Autostrobe tuner rest on cargo containers.

microphones are being made, but I keep putting them up against a lot of the older mics, and the new microphones seldom make the cut—depending on the source, of course." Michael adds, "I always find myself going back to the old tube microphones, especially for vocals and things with low SPL [sound pressure levels]. To me, older microphones have a very specific quality to them, and I like equipment with its own coloration." Still, Michael's love for older pieces such as the Neve mic preamps doesn't preclude his incorporating newer gear. "I also use a few George Massenburg pieces. I have the mixer, compressor, and stereo mastering equalizer. They are all incredible."

Michael's combining of the old with the new is most apparent with his recent transition to digital recording. Previously and to some extent still known for being an analog freak, Michael has tempered his fanaticism by experimenting with digital recording. "My preference right now is to record digitally. The thing is, I am trying to do it as high-end as possible." Michael's system includes the Euphonix R-1 digital hard-disk recorder with 96kHz/24-bit sampling, and Steinberg's Nuendo, a system that was introduced to him by Frank Filipetti (see Chapter 11). "Frank has been a big advocate of the R-1. The first time I tried using it in 96k, Frank wasn't around. I compared it to other decks and it just didn't sound right. The next time we tried it, we used different D/A [digital-to-analog] converters to hone the recorder's sound. With the different D/As it was evident that the R-1 system sounded much better. It has the best aspects of analog—well, with some notable exceptions—but I was most impressed by the fact that it reproduces a sound's transients like nothing I have ever heard before."

The R-1 system's striking sound quality, and its ability to work well with a sound's front end, is one of the main reasons why Michael made the full jump to digi. "When recording on analog tape I noticed that a lot of the harmonics from different sounds would smear. Cymbals, vocals, guitars, hi-hat, the top of the snare drum—they all kind of blend together in this sort of wash. It's hard to pick out the individual instruments." The R-1 is digital, so there isn't any tape compression, and unless the material is recorded without preserving any kind of separation, sounds do not spill over into one another, allowing each individual instrument to pop out. Michael reiterates, "In an idiom where there is a tremendous amount of distortion—guitars, basses, and even in the upper vocal range—it's important for instruments' individual harmonics to be represented adequately."

Despite all of the positive results with the R-1, Michael couldn't put his diehard analog fanaticism to rest. "Analog tape sounds great," he says. "I just don't like the conversion process wherein one goes from analog to digital. I recently tried to A/B the R-1 against an analog deck. The analog's lower sub-bass was perceivable, but instead of kind of warming things, it was adding a fuzz. It doesn't come close to the low end I am getting from the R-1. This was quite disappointing, because I was hoping to combine digital and analog sounds at some point. Instead, analog didn't bring anything to the table. It didn't sound good at all, but I tried. I preferred the R-1 to the analog deck in that instance, but I wouldn't rule out using analog at some point."

Even though Michael has gone over to digital's "dark side," he's quick to note that if people do not know how to use digital recording properly, their results will not adhere to the results he is getting with his setup. "I think in a way the advent of digital technology has hindered the music industry, at least to an extent. Recording with digital technology is different. People think that digital technology is supposed to sound like the source. They believe what they read in ads—that if they take something out of a box, it will sound great. But it won't unless it is used right. A digital system is not like a multitrack tape machine, where you have to clean and demagnetize the heads, set the bias, or whatever. Digital recording is a different medium, and it's a lot harder than it seems. It is a matter of knowing how you are clocking it, what kind of converters you are using, and why you are using them. Musicians have to know so much about it, and they often don't."

Beinhorn's recording studio is symbolic of

The mic and cable closet, which houses Michael's vintage tube mic collection.

a number of technical and economic changes reverberating throughout the music industry. The downturn in CD sales, and the shrinking recording budgets that have accompanied it, are mirrored by radical improvements in digital recording's affordability, accessibility, and sound quality. This heralds a number of fundamental shifts that are beginning to take shape: the empowerment of artists to create professional-level recordings on their own terms, new forms of distribution, and new roles for record labels, artists, and producers. It's unclear exactly how this new business paradigm will develop, and what effect it may have on the overall quality of artists' creative output. A new breed of musician is getting "wired," taking on more of the business and production aspects of making music in their own home studios and in facilities like Michael's Standard Electrical Recorders. A new level of creative freedom and control is opening

A vintage Neve 8028 console with 24 inputs and 32 monitors.

up for artists, with exciting promise for the future of musicianship. But along with this freedom, attention to the nuances of the art of recording is in danger of becoming an afterthought, as is the collection of creative skills and business savvy that the Michael Beinhorns of the world bring to the recording process. This is the exploding and dynamic world of the home studio.

TECH TALK
Tube Mics

Tube mics use vacuum tubes rather than transistors to amplify the signal. Tubes often add a warm, pleasant distortion to the signals they process. Michael Beinhorn's collection of vintage tube mics includes: Neumann U67 and M49; Sony C-37; Telefunken ELA-M251; and AKG C-60, C-12, C-24, and C-28.

Older tube mics have their audiophile fans, but the old parts break and the capacitors dry up, making the mics prone to failure. The big problem with vintage mics is that as time passes, the sound from mic to mic varies more and more. So it's not only a matter of finding an old tube mic, it is finding one that sounds right.

Some manufacturers are trying to recreate the old equipment with today's techniques. Sometimes they can get close to the original sound, but if the new models have a transformer constructed out of different metals, for instance, the overall sound may not be quite the same.

Michael's Serge modular analog synthesizer.

Digital Recording Systems

There are several digital systems out there besides the Euphonix R-1, including Emagic's Logic Audio, MOTU's Digital Performer, and others; Tascam, Fostex, and Mackie also have hard-disk recording systems. They all have recording capabilities, but they are most often used for writing and sequencing. For digital recording in professional studios, Digidesign's Pro Tools has become the standard.

Euphonix R-1 48-channel hard-disk recorder: **www.euphonix.com**

Steinberg Nuendo: **www.steinberg.net**

Michael's Control Room Within A Room

"Initially the room was just wide open—so I changed it to make more of a proper listening area, separate from the outside room. I just wanted a place to hear. The original idea was to enclose the wide space by draping heavy curtains over the sides. Instead I just started hanging blankets, but it actually turned out a lot better than I thought it would. The curtains may have looked a lot nicer than this, but the blankets really deaden the mixing area, making it a type of active area."

An overhead view of Michael's room-within-a-room, including his Neve 8028 console.

Michael's Digital Downfalls

"Every piece of gear has pitfalls," says Beinhorn. "Nothing is perfect. I mean, what Steinberg has done with its Nuendo system is fantastic, and sonically it is a great recording system. But as far as flexibility and 'interfaceability' goes, it could use a few improvements, at least on my end. It's a professional recording system built on a 96k platform, but unfortunately it uses a light pipe instead of Steinberg's own direct AES connection. It's a drag for me to use a different company for the AES card, which fortunately works—but since we are dealing with a lot of tracks, we have to do a lot of internal mixing in the computer. Even though I feel Nuendo is sonically superior to Pro Tools, once you start mixing in the computer you start running into the same sonic problems that you would if you were using a system like Pro Tools alone. You lose the integrity of the sound. The computer starts crunching numbers like crazy, and it starts to get grainy and unpleasant-sounding. Everything you worked very hard to try to create falls by the wayside."

Hooking Up Digital Gear

There are basically three ways to hook up digital equipment: S/PDIF, AES, and fiber optic cable.

S/PDIF (Sony/Philips Digital Interface): S/PDIF uses an RCA-type connector and a single coaxial cable. (TDIF, or Tascam Digital Interface, is a similar format invented by Tascam.) Due to the fact that some consoles, DATs, etc., have both S/PDIF or TDIF as well as AES, they are now easily interchangeable with AES connectors. S/PDIF is

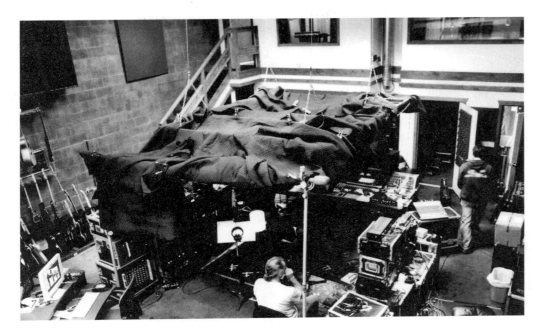

The Standard Electrical Recorders control room and digital editing workstation.

more common than AES in smaller home-recording setups. Note: A common mistake is for musicians to use home stereo cables to hook up digital equipment. In reality, it's necessary to buy a proper cable. A professional cable may cost about $150, but it can transmit the very high-frequency signal more accurately than a cheaper cable.

AES: An AES connector (also called AES/EBU) is similar to an XLR mic connector. It uses a dual coaxial cable with two conductors and a shield.

Fiber optic cable (a.k.a. light pipe): Basically a single plastic or glass thread that can carry many channels, usually eight. No electricity runs through the thread, only light.

When connecting digital equipment, each piece should share the same clock. A single clock source, such as a word-clock generator, should be used to clock the entire studio; otherwise, little clicks and digital errors may be introduced into the signals.

Connecting Analog Gear To Digital Gear

An A/D converter samples an analog signal and converts it within a processor to a series of digital values to represent the signal. There are various A/Ds: flash, half flash, integrator, delta sigma or modulator, successive approximation, and voltage-to-frequency.

To interface analog to digital, use an A-to-D converter, a D-to-A converter, or both. Simply plug them in. Digital goes in and analog comes out, or vice versa. No clocking is needed between these two worlds.

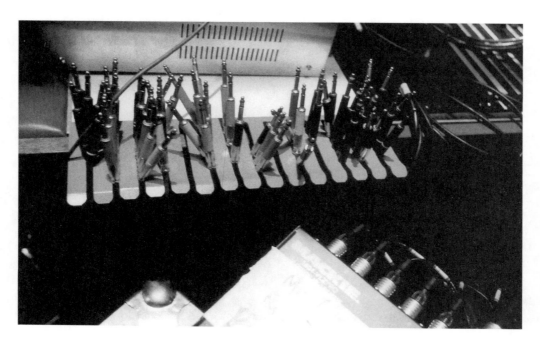

TT cables for routing signals through patch bays.

AROUND THE CIRCUIT

Harmonic distortion occurs when two or more frequencies are present at the same time. When they interact, some of the harmonics are pleasant as when a pianist plays a major chord, but some are grating, as when a violinist rubs the bow against the grain on the highest string. Generally, distortion sounds warmer in tube circuits than in transistors, and warmer in analog systems than in digital.

Michael's Neve 1057 preamps use what is known as **Class A** circuit topology. The electronics in Class A gear are cleaner, partly because the sound passes through fewer components than in a **Class B** amplifier, making the Class A more desirable to buy and use.

A **mastering EQ** is usually calibrated exactly, with small steps for each frequency band— sometimes 0.5dB for each click of the controls. It is used primarily for final mixes, but can really be used anywhere.

The Tube Tech SMC 2A is a compressor that can split the signal into lows, midrange, and highs, and compress each band separately.

Sampling Rates

CDs normally use a 44.1kHz sampling rate, which has been a standard (along with 48kHz) for a while. Today's higher sampling rates (e.g., 96kHz with 24-bit resolution) are more accurate for recording, especially in the high-frequency range. Basically, the higher the sampling rate, the more accurate the recording. The top systems now can do 192kHz.

Michael's Console

"I have the Neve 8028 with 24 ins and 32 monitors, set up as a big monitor. We are doing all of our bussing and mixing with this little portable George Massenburg GML 9100 mixer." Michael records through his mixer and uses the Neve as a monitoring system to hear everything.

Chapter Two

Sonic Youth
New York, New York

"This studio has really revitalized the way we record. It has been one of the greatest things that ever happened to us."

SONIC YOUTH IS ONE of the few bands that has managed to attain rock-icon status not only within the indie-rock echelons, but also within the music-press elite and the music community at large. The band's ability to command respect on so many levels is perhaps due to the members' unconventional approach to music. Creatively, they have practically built an entire genre around the concept of free-form dissonant experimentalism. Commercially, they are one of the few bands to keep their indie "street cred," retaining creative control of their music releases even after moving from independent

A view of Sonic Youth's tetragonal live room with Steve Shelley's plywood drum platform on the left.

labels (Neutral, Homestead, SST, Sub Pop, Blast First) to the major label DGC (now Interscope/Geffen/A&M, under the umbrella of Universal Music). Sonic Youth's avant-garde musicality and band-to-business savvy have made them the poster children for eccentric musicians everywhere, crafting music without any set precedents while breaking through the taboos associated with working for a major label. The band's premise of deconstructing music into noise—or vice versa, constructing noise into music—further underlines their allegiance to the drive and spirit of making music over the tedium of perfecting music. The pitch-perfect precision found on many of today's CDs is nowhere to be found on SY's recordings, and this disregard for convention is characterized by the way they work within Echo Canyon Studios.

Sonic Youth's modified Neve 51-series 36-channel mixing console with an open slot for a 12-channel bucket.

The hallways and storage room adjacent to Sonic Youth's live room.

Murray Street—the address of Sonic Youth's Echo Canyon Studio—is situated in the heart of New York's Tribeca district. The outside of the four-story building is unremarkable in appearance, but upon reaching the cargo elevator, Sonic Youth's atypical rumblings gradually begin to resonate through the walls. The elevator doors open to the fourth floor almost directly in front of the band's control room. There, a leviathan modified Neve 51 Series mixing console takes center stage. Several wires and cables are strewn across one 12-channel bucket of the board as the bandmembers make a few additional adjustments to the console (see section on the modified board, page 28). Above the Neve, a monitor displays what looks like a collage of home movies. On the screen, a very young Thurston Moore is visibly out of his comfort zone, not playing guitar but flailing on the drums "Animal"-style. Aaron Mullan, Sonic Youth's studio

"My original Tele Deluxe had an ƒ-hole in it—and after our gear was stolen in '99, a guy [Saul Koll] from Portland built me another guitar with similar modifications on it. He put the ƒ-hole back in because it was such a trademark of mine at the time." —Lee Ranaldo

The entryway to Echo Canyon.

engineer, explains that he is transferring all of Sonic Youth's old VHS tapes to digital for possible use on a few forthcoming DVD releases. Across the hallway is the large tetragonal live room. In the back section of the wall-to-wall-carpeted space sits Steve Shelley's drum kit, a 1968 Ludwig with Blue Oyster finish that's been retrofitted with Yamaha hardware (see sidebar, page 34). Underneath his kit is a plywood platform built to boost the drum sound and give the otherwise dead room a bit of a "kick." Aaron explains, "Since Steve's drums are the only acoustic instrument in the band, the room is part of his instrument. Steve has been very involved in working to improve the room's sound." Sonic Youth has installed wood floors and walls in the drum sec-

---

ECHO CANYON STUDIO

"When you are a band that works like we do, you put a lot of time in rehearsal. After 22 years, we have found that we get to hear a lot of beautiful things that no one else but us hears. Maybe they are on cassette somewhere, and maybe one or two pieces get released somewhere, but it's mostly the four of us in the studio just saying, 'Wow, that was amazing'" —Lee Ranaldo

---

Lee Ranaldo of Sonic Youth.

tion of the room; they have angled the walls, constructed isolating risers, and placed acoustical foam in key places, all to improve the acoustics for the drums. Kim Gordon (bassist and guitarist) and Jim O'Rourke (producer and musician-of-all-trades) have a few of their amps and heads stacked against the opposite side of the wall. Everything is arranged as if prepped for an impromptu session. Beyond the live room is another narrow hall, which opens up into a two large closets filled with numerous road cases, guitar cases, and odd bits of old gear: 4-tracks, reel-to-reels, an old pair of Scully ½" 2-track machines, cassette recorders, and the like. Lee Ranaldo, Sonic Youth's guitarist, makes sense of Echo Canyon's intangible organization. "This whole place is very 'seat of the pants.' The way we work in the studio is kind of by trial and error. We make it work for us."

In accordance with such idiosyncratic mannerisms, Sonic Youth uses Echo Canyon Studios as an extension of their unhinged creative process as well as a place to easily record their material as it takes form. Lee continues, "There is a vibe that happens when we are writing and playing that we can never quite recreate, and we like to have those unique moments caught on tape. That was basically the whole impetus for setting up the studio." Not known for songs with verse-chorus-verse structures, Sonic Youth often creates ideas during jams or spur-of-the-moment sparks of creativity, with a single bar often transforming into an entire section of a song. "We'll just get together to shape songs and kick things around until something starts to happen,"

Lee says. "Sometimes we're working on something and a half an hour later we think, That was a cool moment—how can we expand on it?"

Sonic Youth has a way of transforming even the most mundane recording techniques into sonic experimentation, and this creative fluidity makes it essential for the band to have some method for documenting their ideas. From their first days playing together, their solution has been to record all of their rehearsals and sessions. At the time, this meant making simple cassette-tape recordings, which the group used as

---

KEYS ON GUITARS

"We normally write the tuning on the back of the necks or headstocks so we don't forget the guitars' tunings. At this point our touring crew takes care of so much stuff, we don't remember the tuning of every song. If you asked us the tuning for a particular song, it would take us a bit to remember it." —Lee Ranaldo

---

An Ampex ATR-100 ½" 2-track machine and its remote panel.

Electro-Voice RE-20 and AKG D-112 microphones.

creative sketchpads. The sketchpad process is still an essential part of Sonic Youth's recording technique, and the decision to take on Echo Canyon Studios was driven by their innate desire to create on an extemporaneous level. Lee explains, "At a certain point, I believe, after we headlined the '95 Lollapalooza tour and we had a little more cash, we decided to set up a studio that was a little more hi-fi than our basic cassette-tape or 8-track way of doing things. We also wanted to have a mic on everyone's amp

---

WORKING OUTSIDE THE LABEL

"In early '99, we received some letters about a young fan of ours who committed suicide. I forget exactly how it came about, but we ended up doing a record for the San Francisco Suicide Hotline. We recorded the material with Wharton Tiers, one of our producers. It was all feedback: Thurston and I put all of our guitars in the playing room leaning up against the amps. There was this insane amount of noise going on while we were recording. I think we recorded the feedback for about an hour. Then we chopped it up into tracks and did more stuff with it, and we released it through this San Francisco independent distribution company. It was called the Silver Sessions, and I think it generated something like $50,000 for the Suicide Hotline. That was very cool. You know, if you have your own studio, you can work on the projects you want to work on." —Lee Ranaldo

---

Lee Ranaldo in the control room.

and be able to solo each channel if we so desired." Echo Canyon is definitely a step above the 8-track, but it's still modest enough for the band to feel comfortable creating with their avant-garde aesthetics.

Sonic Youth has always made a point of creating unique sounds by dissecting their instruments and equipment—perhaps a lost art form in the modern recording world. As one of the few bands to fully embrace modification by tearing apart the pots and wires of guitars and taking an almost cavalier approach to the placement and selection of pickups, they have revitalized the art of creating new sounds through guitar modification. (See guitar customizing, page 37.) A Sonic Youth guitar is not only a creative outlet for songwriting, it's also a creative outlet in terms of its construction. Thurston's Drifter (a guitar that was unfortunately stolen in 1999) was essentially a completely redesigned instrument. He tore out the frets, strung the guitar with four bass strings, and then added a few drumsticks—all basically for one song, "Eric's Trip." Sonic Youth's guitars are not always meant to be kept in a pristine state, as dismantling them opens an entire realm of sonic exploration.

In addition to reconstructing guitars to discover new sounds, Sonic Youth has made a point of experimenting with various tape formats and tape speeds when recording. "There was a time when we would fool around with things a little more," explains Lee. "During the recording of *Dirty*, we spent a good deal of time with Butch Vig experimenting with tape speeds—recording the same passage first at 30 IPS and then at 15 IPS on the multitrack, and then mixing each down first at 30

CLASSIC SOUNDS OF THE 16-TRACK

"Layla and other albums from that period just sound great. I think 16-track recorders were a big part of the reason why. The machines were sophisticated enough to allow artists to capitalize on all the recording breakthroughs that people like the Beatles had initiated, yet still limited enough to allow the music's freshness to come through with immediacy. Later, as 24- and 48-track media became the standard, musicians began to spend too much time fussing over the little things and began to use too many tracks for overdubbing. Of course, it worked for some records—but I think as a rule the limits of 16-track recorders were actually very effective. If you look at the track sheets they included in Layla, you can see how creative the engineers were about fitting each sound onto the available tracks. You'd have one track that had percussion in one part of the song, backing vocals in another, and a lead guitar in a third section! That kind of creative recording really enhanced the final product." —Lee Ranaldo

and then at 15 to see what sounded best. At the time we preferred 15 IPS for both multitrack and mixdown." (See section on recording *Dirty*, page 30.) *Dirty* became one of Sonic Youth's most distinctive-sounding records, benefiting from "the classic way of experimenting and perfecting." Sonic Youth still experiments with varying tape speeds and sounds, but with Jim O'Rourke's introduction into the band as a producer and full-fledged member, they have for the most part returned to recording at 30 IPS, settling on the format as the one with the least tape hiss and most clarity on the high end. (This nod to fidelity seems to dovetail with the band's recent practice of editing some tracks on Pro Tools for editing. The sonic precision of 30-IPS tracking seems to fit better with digital editing than the deliberately low-fi luster of 15 IPS.)

Tracking is another nuts-and-bolts recording fundamental that Sonic Youth uses as a creative rallying point. Instead of building songs as pieces—tracking drums, bass, guitar, vocals, overdubs, etc.—Sonic Youth prefers to track live. Lee explains the benefits: "Tracking live is really what it is all about for us—the all-together live playing experience. We don't wear headphones, except for Steve, and we normally don't use a lot of baffling. We're basically all playing together in one room." Due to the ambient bleeding that happens when tracking live in one room, most professional recordings are done with some combination of isolation booths, separate takes, and sonic separation of the instruments—yet for Sonic Youth, a more basic recording approach provides more room to experiment. Lee continues, "The way we track live is pretty loud and there is definitely a lot of bleed and such, but we would much

REASONS FOR THE JAZZMASTER

"Thurston and I buy Jazzmasters whenever we see a deal on them. Usually if they are original they are very expensive. Sometimes Jazzmasters that have been refinished or redone are worth nothing to collectors, so we can buy them really cheap. We couldn't care less about the bodies; we treat the guitars pretty bad anyway. We just like the Jazzmaster shape and the size of the neck, as well as the tremolo bar—it's simple and gets the right effect. There's no tremolo lock-down [a mechanism that clamps the strings in place to keep them more in tune] or fancy stuff like that on the Jazzmasters, but that's okay. We hate locking tuners; they are just too fussy, and we are all about tunings and often need to re-tune quickly. Plus, going out of tune occasionally is part of our reality. It keeps it real." —Lee Ranaldo

rather have everybody listening to each other naturally than be working with the amps in the iso booths, where we don't have direct access to them and where we are working off headphone mixes. That is just too sterile. I mean, how are we supposed to rock out in that situation? It's just too messed up for our style." Lee expands a bit more on the logistics of tracking in their live space: "Except for the changes we made in Steve's section of the room, the room itself is not super-loud; it is actually fairly dead. So we can get everyone in there without building up a huge mass of sound."

Miking Sonic Youth's live room is a straightforward process, but it's done in a way that allows room for sonic exploits. "We basically go in there looking to get great sound out of our amps, so we don't spend a whole lot of time on miking. For instance, we don't go in and put ten different mics on one amp, or try to figure out which one sounds best by putting the mic at five, ten, then 20 feet away. At times it's beneficial to put up a room mic, but we generally prefer to close-mic every-thing." (See section on open- vs. close-miking, page 31.) The back-to-basics essence of tracking live goes hand-in-hand with Sonic's free-flowing vibe, as does their approach to effects and gear. One gets the feeling that having to rely on outboard gear would ultimately be too proper for the band. "We don't have an effects-laden studio," says Lee. "We have a few compressors and some reverbs, but other than that we prefer to get the sound ourselves, getting the stuff onto tape natural and mixing it so it sounds natural."

The creating and recording freedom that Echo Canyon provides has not only enhanced Sonic Youth's fluid work aesthetics, it's also stepped up their creative out-put, and as a result has opened up new avenues for the band to release its music. By capturing more impromptu and experimental sessions—all recorded at professional quality—the band quickly generated a backlog of material not necessarily suited for Geffen. Lee describes the steps that led toward releasing material on their own. "Once we had this amazing multitrack system, we were in here all of the time working—either on solo projects, or just for fun. We were creating so much amazing material that we wanted to put it out there."

To get this new music out onto the market, Steve Shelley created his own label, Smells Like Records; Sonic Youth as a whole created the SYR Series, a succession of albums highlighting the band's more eclectic musicianship. For a band that normally puts out a record about every two years on Geffen/Interscope, the numerous releases in the SYR Series helped Sonic Youth reach many of its diehard devotees who see every show and want to hear more than the major-label material. Lee explains the importance of creating SYR: "It was a great way for us to reach our more hardcore fans. The series took off and sold quite a bit. People really responded to those releases and heard yet another level of the band." Along the lines of the SYR series, Sonic Youth has also participated in other one-off releases like the *Silver Sessions* for the

Joni Mitchell's picture rests atop a Studer A-800 Mk III 2" 16-track.

San Francisco Suicide Hotline, with proceeds going to the charity. Sonic Youth's unique arrangement with Geffen helped them bypass many of the legal pitfalls associated with side projects and sub-labels. Lee continues, "We have been able to construct this unique deal and relationship with Geffen. They never get on our case with all of our side projects or small releases—plus, it probably wasn't material they would want to release anyway. The SYR stuff was pretty easy to get off the ground. It was no problem for anyone involved." Sonic Youth's labels, SYR and Smells Like Records, illustrate yet another way they have made the most of their investment in Echo Canyon Studios.

Economic and fiscal factors also had a more practical influence on Sonic Youth's decision to upgrade their old 8-track system to a pro-quality multitrack setup. "We were sick of being in studios that cost $1,000-plus a day, and being on the clock, so to speak. It didn't make sense for a band like us that records the way we do." By having a pro setup at Echo Canyon, they could cut out the costs of recording in commercial studios. Lee clarifies Sonic Youth's monetary reasoning: "Given that we are still on a major label, we still get fairly decent recording budgets. We realized that instead of

Studio Equipment

Console:

Neve 51 Series 36-channel custom mixing console modified by Dominick Constanzo and Tim Glasgow

Mic preamps:

Great River MP-4

API 3124

Sytek MPX-4A (2)

Drawmer 1960

Tape machines:

Studer A-800 Mk III 2" 16-track

Ampex ATR 100 $\frac{1}{2}$" 2-track restored by ATR Services

Digital Recording:

Pro Tools TDM system

Outboard gear:

UREI 1176 compressor

Universal Audio/UREI LA-4 (4)

Summit Audio DCL-200 dual compressor/limiter

Manley Massive Passive stereo tube EQ

Demeter RV-1 Real Reverb

Lexicon PCM 70

Little Labs IBP Junior

Sample list of microphones:

Neumann U47

Neumann KM184 (2)

Royer R121 (2)

STC 4038

AKG C-414 (2)

AKG D-112

AKG C-451E

Sennheiser 421 (3)

Shure SM7 (4)

Shure SM57 (4)

putting money into a commercial studio for a month or so, we could sink our recording budget into gear and create our own facility." Sonic Youth's budgetary reasoning illustrates what could be a new economic model for band recording. "A year's worth of New York rent costs about the same as going into a commercial studio for a month. Our rent is the biggest part of our expenses here, because it's a New York City loft—but in the end, even with all of our maintenance and our very few gear purchases, everything pays for itself over time. It just works out far better and it's more realistic for a band like us that is not making scads and scads of money. It's a way around the traditional recording system."

Over the span of its recording career, Sonic Youth has grown from being über-indie 8-track advocates to being über-indie rock icons. Echo Canyon Studios has allowed them to step up their recording capabilities while still maintaining their unconventional rock aesthetics and never fully letting go of their home-core techniques. Their studio is not some kind of rock-star glam project; it's a place specifically designed so the band can feel as comfortable as possible developing its unique style of music. Lee sums it up: "This studio has really revitalized the way we like to record. It has been one of the greatest things that ever happened to us. That said, we started out with an 8-track system, so we know that it doesn't matter if a studio has every piece of gear in the world or if it has two shitty microphones and a Roland tape recorder. What matters is the music. There are so many ways people can record music at the moment. Just take it and make it work for you. That has always been our aesthetic—in a way, more so today than ever."

TECH TALK
Modifying Sonic Youth's Neve 51 Series Console

"This board has come a long way since we first brought it about two years ago," says Lee Ranaldo of the 36-channel Neve 51 Series console at Echo Canyon. "We have been going through it quite extensively. [NYC technician] Dominick Constanzo and our longtime friend/tech Tim Glasgow are doing a lot of the modifications. At the moment we have 36 channels that are arranged in buckets—but we have one more bucket of 12 that we may want to hook in to make it a 48-channel board, which would be very beneficial for us. We have also been recapping every single channel, doing a lot of modifi-

(Clockwise from left) Echo Canyon's control room; outboard gear including a few Universal Audio/UREI LA-4s and a Summit Audio DCL-200 dual compressor/limiter; a vintage Korg synthesizer.

cations to bring it back to what we need. In addition, we've spent some time building out the pan system. It's all back-moded to a stereo console." Many of the extensive modifications were necessary because the board was built by Neve as a film mixing console, capable of Dolby surround-sound but not simple stereo mixes. Dominick has been working on a number of additional mods to the board, including a new master section. Lee has been pleased with the results: "It's an ongoing process, but the board is definitely sounding better and better all the time."

A **bucket** is a segment of a modular console that individual channel modules drop into. Some have eight to a segment and some have 12, while others have the whole board as one big bucket.

Adding buckets is a complicated process, especially for vintage boards. The buckets must be physically attached and then wired. Some boards can be expanded with cable extensions, but new boards are usually set up to require add-on parts.

Recapping means replacing the capacitors. The heat inside a board speeds up

Sonic Youth's studio archive of music on 2" and ½" tape.

aging, and the capacitors dry up over time, so they eventually have to be replaced. New capacitors often do improve the sound; at the very least, they bring the board back to sounding new. Capacitors manufactured today are better quality, so they don't need to be replaced as often.

Down & Dirty Recording Tips

"For our album *Dirty* we were working with Butch Vig [drummer/producer for Garbage] at the Magic Shop in New York, right after he had produced Nirvana's *Nevermind*," says Lee Ranaldo. "We began experimenting with 24-track and 16-track tape machines. For the most part, we ended up using 16-track because the tape is wider, which gave us the best sound quality for an analog format. A lot of classic rock records of the '70s, like *Layla*, were recorded on 16-track, when it was still considered new technology. Hearing the deluxe edition of that record really shows how they used the 16-track to record. Those old albums sound great—and I think the 16-track was a big part of the reason why (See page 25).

"When we began to record *Dirty*, a friend and eventually a producer of ours, Wharton Tiers, began telling us about the benefits of recording on slower tape speeds. Even though you get more hiss, the bottom end gets fatter, so we thought we would try it. Most people record on 24 tracks at 30 IPS (inches per second). We decided to record with the 16-track and then began playing around with different combinations. For instance, we would record on 16-track at 15 IPS and mix to ½" inch tape at 15 IPS, and then we'd mix the same passage to ½" tape at 30 IPS. Following that, we would record additional material at 30 IPS, mix it to ½" at 15 IPS, and then mix it at 30 IPS. We were just trying to find what worked for us—what our ears liked best. It was the first time we really spent time investigating the possibilities before jumping into the actual recording process."

24-/16-Track Tape & Recording Speed Basics

The wider each track is, the less hiss there will be relative to the recorded signal. On a 2" tape with 24 tracks, each track is skinnier than on a 16-track recording using the same 2" tape. With 16 tracks, each track is wider and therefore has less hiss.

At faster tape speeds the top end is better, but the bottom end gets a bit thinner.

An ATR-100 ½" 2-track machine recently restored by ATR Services.

Recording at 15 IPS gives a better bottom end than 30 IPS but offers less transparency on top—and more hiss.

It's all a juggling act. Today some engineers are mixing onto 2" tape with only eight tracks, so each track is really wide at nearly ¼". (The tracks are not quite ¼" wide, as there has to be a bit of room between the tracks.) This format is being used as an archival method for surround mixes. It provides the same amount of tape width per channel as a stereo mix on ½" analog.

There's now a 1" stereo ATR machine going around, which means it has even wider tracks for analog sound (½" per track) with little hiss. Those mixes should sound great!

Close-Miking Vs. Open-Miking

While tracking, Sonic Youth often brings the mics as close as possible to their amps and drums (known as close-miking). At times, they move their mics back to get more of the room's ambient sound (open-miking). Open-miking allows the recording to capture more of each amp's or instrument's sound, but the downside is that a guitar could end up in the drum mics, for example—and if the guitar bleeds too much or needs to be retracked, it can be problematic. With Sonic Youth's live tracking setup, they close-mic most of the time to avoid undesired ambient noise.

Tracking With Tape & Pro Tools

Sonic Youth normally records on the multitrack tape machine and then locks the tape to Pro Tools for additional overdubs and ease of editing. For vocals, the band tracks straight to Pro Tools, but in general the ability to combine analog's Old School warmth

Bitter rivals: Sonic Youth's Pro Tools editing system and Neve mixing console.

and ambience with Pro Tools' advanced editing capabilities allows Sonic Youth to maintain its analog aesthetics while still keeping up with today's digital sensibilities. Lee explains that even though they use Pro Tools for editing, they remain ardent analog fans. "Our setup works for us. It is probably a bit bulkier than other people's, and it makes recording more expensive, that's for sure—the tape costs a lot more than just the hard drive. Even though analog is more expensive, analog is still the way we like to work, and it's how we will continue to work as long as it remains cost-effective."

SONIC YOUTH'S GEAR

Favorite mics: "Our microphone collection is fairly modest, not super atomic," says Lee Ranaldo. "We have an assortment of both new and old, but it leans more toward modern mics just because the Old School mics are so expensive. We have a few older models such as an old Coles 4038 and a really expensive Neumann U47. The 47 is by far our best, most expensive, and favorite mic—but every mic is interesting to some degree. Our present plan for the studio is to expand our microphone closet."

Coles 4038s: Ribbon mics that sound great on horns, guitar amps, and even drum overheads. These low-output mics deliver a smooth top end that's not too "trebly." Originally designed by the BBC and manufactured in the U.K. as the STC 4038, the vintage mic was reissued by Coles under its own name; people generally refer to these mics as "Coles."

Neumann U47s: Tube mics originally made by Telefunken. Neumann has been making an FET (Field Effect Transistor) model for quite a while now; it's usually called an "FET 47" as opposed to a "tube 47."

Steve's drum setup: "Steve always has the kick drum, snare, three toms, hi-hat, one crash, and one ride," explains Aaron Mullan, Sonic Youth's studio engineer. "Sometimes a ride sizzle is added as a second ride. The gongs are mounted on a rack behind Steve or to his side. The clay drums are only for specific songs and are not used often. Steve uses Remo coated Ambassador heads, except for the beater-side kick-drum head, which is a Remo Pinstripe. When recording certain songs, Steve replaces one of the drums with a piece from a '60s Gretsch kit he keeps here. For any given song, Steve will add or remove tape from the top heads or rearrange the damp- ening on the kick head, and he'll experiment with different cymbals to suit the song."

Sonic Youth's Guitars

Aaron Mullan describes Sonic Youth's guitars and how the band maintains a semblance of order with so many different models. For Sonic Youth's complete gear history, as compiled by Chris Lawrence, go to **www.sonicyouth.com/mustang/eq/gear.html***.*

Sonic Youth's guitar basics: At the studio we have about 40 "active" guitars and basses on hand, plus another 20 or so hanging around. We tour with about 30. At the beginning of each tour, the band comes up with a song list of what they would like to play, and then we figure out what instruments will be needed. In general, each guitar has a unique tuning. Often each guitar stays in that tuning for years, but some-

Steve Shelley's custom-built drum space.

Steve Shelley's Drums

1960s Ludwig kit retrofitted with Yamaha hardware and otherwise fine-tuned by the drummaker Nodar Rode:

22x14 kick drum (w/Yamaha mounting hardware)

Ludwig chrome snare

12x8 rack tom (w/Yamaha mounting hardware)

13x9 rack tom (w/Yamaha mounting hardware)

16x16 floor tom (w/Yamaha mounting hardware)

Selection of: Zildjian Constantinople Light Ride 20" or Zildjian Custom Dark Ride sizzle 20"

Selection of: Zildjian Custom Dark Crash 17", Zildjian Custom Dark Crash 16", Zildjian K Dark Crash Medium Thin 15", Zildjian K Dark Crash Medium Thin 16", Zildjian K Dark Crash 17", or Zildjian Constantinople Crash 16"

Selection of: Zildjian Custom Dark hi-hats or Zildjian K hi-hats

Additional pieces:

Zildjian Boa gong 10"

Chinese gong 12"

Chinese gong 10"

Pearl snare stand

Yamaha cymbal stands

Pearl drum throne

DW 5000 hi-hat stand

DW 5000 kick-drum pedal with custom beater

Moroccan clay drum (large)

Moroccan clay drum (small)

Various maracas

Small bells

Pro-Mark TWJZX drumsticks

Felt mallets

times we'll change the tuning on a guitar that has not been used for a while—either to play a new song or an old one, if the guitar for that song has been lost, stolen, destroyed, or retuned. [Sonic Youth's equipment was stolen from a show in 1999. If you have any information on the missing models, go to **www.sonicyouth.com**.]

Fender Jazzmasters: The guitar most identified with Sonic Youth is the Fender Jazzmaster. Some have said Lee and Thurston, along with J Mascis of Dinosaur Jr., repopularized this guitar in the '80s. Lee and Thurston prefer old Jazzmasters—partly because the necks on the early-'60s models are easier to play, and partly due to the fact that they look for guitars that are physically trashed. They figure they will trash the guitars anyway, so they don't care about condition. When Sonic Youth buys a Jazzmaster, the first thing we do is rip out all the knobs and switches except for the pickup selector and the volume knob. If the guitar is for Thurston, the bridge saddle gets replaced with a Gibson Tune-o-Matic. If the guitar is for Lee, the Jazzmaster pickups are replaced with humbucker pickups from a Fender Telecaster Deluxe, and the saddle is replaced with a Fender Mustang saddle. The saddles get replaced because the stock Jazzmaster saddle allows the strings to jump around when struck too hard. (After the mods have been done to a Lee guitar we call it a "Jazzblaster," which is Lee's own design. We actually tried to get Fender to make them that way; they seemed interested at first, but they haven't done anything with that idea yet.) Before the guitar can be played, the bridge is taken apart and the tremolo arm is made to stay in place with a cable tie. This way the tremolo arm can support the guitar's weight as it is held and shaken. (Years before Lee put Tele Deluxe pickups in all of his Jazzmaster bodies, he played Tele Deluxes much of the time. He still plays them live for old songs.)

Fender Mustangs & Jaguars: The band also owns several Fender Mustangs and Jaguars. These guitars also get most of the electronics ripped out except for just the pickup selector and a volume knob. The Jaguar currently in the studio was also modified to have a Mustang saddle.

Drifter: Another iconic Sonic Youth guitar is the Drifter, which has been in the band's arsenal for 20 years. In the '80s Thurston basically redesigned his Drifter by tearing out the frets, stringing the guitar with four bass strings, placing two drum-

A small sample of Sonic Youth's huge guitar collection.

sticks under the strings, and using an obscure tuning—*BBF#F#* (low to high)—specifically for "Eric's Trip." Unfortunately, the guitar was stolen in 1999. In 2000, Sonic tech Eric Baecht made a new model similar to the original; Sonic calls it the Drifter II.

Recent guitars: Thurston still plays mostly Jazzmasters. The main ones he uses are an early-'60s black model that he has had for a few years, and another early-'60s model that he received as a gift from Patti Smith; it was spray-painted gold at some point.

Lee still plays his Jazzblasters and also a new Fender baritone guitar called a Subsonic. He is also into custom guitars made by the Saul Koll company based in Portland, Oregon (**www.kollguitars.com**). These are semi-hollow with an *f*-hole, like the Tele Deluxe Lee was known for, but in the shape of a Jazzmaster—they have Tele Deluxe pickups.

"We have an Ampex ATR model 100 ¹/₂" machine that was recently completely refurbished by this place in Pennsylvania, ATR Services. It was totally beat up and had all of these problems, but it was such a great machine, it was totally worth all of that work and all of that money we put into it. For us, the ATR 100 ¹/₂" machine is great for mixdown—it is the best way to send material off to be mastered. We aren't worried about hiss and stuff. So we are really happy. It is fantastic." —Lee Ranaldo

Deep within Echo Canyon's live room.

Kim Gordon's basses and guitars: Kim uses a Gibson EB-0 bass; sometimes for recording she uses a Gibson Thunderbird or Fender Precision. Her guitars have not been modified much. Instead of ripping out controls, she tends to tape over them so they won't move. Her main guitars are a Les Paul Junior, an Ibanez Talman, and a mysterious thing called the Eterna.

Jim O'Rourke's basses and guitars: Jim was using a Gibson EB-2 bass; he is now using the EB-0 or the Thunderbird on a more regular basis. For guitars Jim has been using an old Tele Deluxe with a Bigsby bridge, a Gibson SG with a Bigsby, one of Lee's Blasters, and sometimes a Music Man StingRay.

STEVE ALBINI'S GUITAR

"Steve Albini made us a 16-string guitar out of old cannibalized pieces of guitars he had sitting around. The guitar has 16 high-E strings on it, so it is quite a 'soprano' guitar. Steve made a penis head on the front of the guitar and called it the Sonic 16. I don't think we've ever used it, but it is definitely cool to have around. Someday we will use it, that's for sure." —Lee Ranaldo

---

One of Sonic Youth's more unusual custom-made guitars.

Sonic's Guitar Customization

"We have always been pretty hard on our instruments, and since all of the electronics inside the guitar are fragile and delicate, they constantly fell apart," says Lee. "Eventually we got into the habit of just taking out all of the electronics. Today on an electric guitar we basically like two pickups and a regular toggle switch."

Guitar Tunings:

Sonic Youth's tunings are some of the most obscure around. In many cases the band has one guitar for a specific tuning, which is labeled on the back. Normally that guitar stays in that tuning until Sonic retires the instrument or starts to use it for a different song. Here are just a few of Sonic's tunings (all low to high) on various guitars:

Thurston's Fender (Black) Jazzmaster,
CGDGBB: "Free City Rhymes," "Renegade Princess," "Sunday," "Hoarfrost"
CGDGCD: "Sympathy for the Strawberry," "The Empty Page," "Disconnection Notice," "Karen Revisited," "Rain on Tin"

Thurston's Blue Strat Copy,
F#F#F#F#EB: "World Looks Red," "Starpower," "Death to Our Friends," "Shadow of a Doubt," "Burning Spear"

Lee's Fender (Green) Jazzmaster,
GGDDD#D#: "Kill Yr Idols," "Brother James," "Kotton Krown"
GGDDFF, "Mote" substitute for
F#F#F#F#EB: "Kool Thing"
F#F#GGAA: "White Kross," "Drunken Butterfly"
DDDDAA: "Schizophrenia," "Catholic Block"

Lee's Gibson Les Paul Deluxes,
GGCGCD: "Bull in the Heather," "Starfield Road"

Kim's Yamaha Pacifica, DADGGB: "Female Mechanic," "Karen Koltrane"

Kim's Gibson Les Paul Junior,
EEBBF#F#: "Sympathy for the Strawberry," "Eric's Trip"; also used by Jim for "Shadow of a Doubt"

Jim's Fender (Sunburst) Mustang,
DFCDFF: "NYC Ghosts and Flowers"

Amps: In the studio Thurston has been using a Fender Prosonic. Live, Thurston uses a Peavey Roadmaster with a Marshall 4x12 cabinet.

For years, Lee used a modified blackface Fender Super Reverb; recently he has been using a handmade Italian amplifier called the Orlando Moby Dick. He also uses a '60s 1x12 amp made by Ampeg for the Giulietti accordion company. Live, Lee plays a Fender Bassman head with a Mesa/Boogie 4x12 cabinet.

In the studio, Kim has been using a '60s Fender Princeton and a '50s Fender Deluxe. Live, Kim uses a Peavey Rockmaster with two Fender 2x12 cabinets.

In the studio, Jim has been using the same guitar amps as Kim. Live, Jim plays through a Mesa/Boogie Mark III.

For bass, Kim and Jim share a new Ampeg SVT-2PRO with an Ampeg 4x10 cabinet.

Thurston Moore's Peavey Roadmaster head.

Lee Ranaldo's handmade Orlando Moby Dick studio amp.

Tone/volume control: "We normally take out the tone controls first, because they are basically useless for the kind of music we play. It just adds another circuit to the line. By eliminating the tone circuitry—especially on particular guitars—you get a slightly nicer sound because the sound has to travel through fewer wires. We also take out the tone control because if it's not all the way up, it just sounds muffled and weird. Occasionally people will use that as an effect, but we prefer just to take it out— we never back off the tone control, or the volume, for that matter! The volume knob is just an on/off switch as far as we're concerned. When it's up all the way, it sounds right. When it's turned down, it starts to get muffley. We just use it to stop the feedback when we're not playing."

Fans and guitar addicts building guitars for Sonic: "A lot of people know that we kind of do funky stuff with our guitars, so they build us all kinds of custommade models. A guy in Germany [Frank Demiel] built me a 12-string guitar with a

Jazzmaster body, old Dan Armstrong lipstick pickups that can be single-coil or double-coil, and a different pickup behind the bridge. It also has a huge kind of Leslie setting that you just push on and off. On top of everything else, it is beautifully made. It is a really cool guitar. It's called a Bullet."

Three-guitar experiments: "We have been experimenting with the three-guitar thing for a while," Lee continues. "On *Washing Machine* there are two or three songs that Kim plays guitar on—no bass. We kind of moved forward from that point. It came to a head when we were making *New York City Ghosts & Flowers*. We thought, Wow, this is a really cool sound—but at the same time we thought it was too bad that we lost bottom frequencies without the bass. When we brought Jim O'Rourke on board to mix that record, we asked him to put some bass on some of those songs. That's what led to him being in the band. Now we basically work with three guitars and bass—sometimes Kim is playing bass, sometimes Jim. We have yet to do a song with two basses, but I am hoping we will. That would be very cool."

Chapter Three

BT

Los Feliz, California

"You would sell your car to buy some of those sounds."

HAVING RECENTLY MOVED from Encino to the Los Angeles suburb Los Feliz, BT is in transition. Known predominantly as an electronic whizoid who harbors clusters of gear and computers and creates lush but technically complex compositions, BT is now toying with a new home-studio setup. BT's cluttered former working environment, with its loads of gear and wires, has been replaced with software, virtual instruments, and host computers. His new digital audio workstations (or DAWs), combined with Virtual Studio Technology (VST, a term coined by Steinberg Technologies), offer a reflective contrast to his former studio.

BT's new Los Feliz space may be sparse, but according to BT it is ten times more powerful than his Encino installation: It's much more efficient, and it's a step toward the super-studio of the future, where everything is "in-house" within the computer. All-digital recording is somewhat new to BT, who has a slick knack for experimenting with the latest pieces of gear and has been known for producing music with a hands-on synth approach. He explains why he is going through a transformation: "It's a great time for me to talk about the changes in my recording setup. I'm in a really cool period of flux. I feel that I am turning a corner that I'm not coming back from." This digi-centric change, perhaps catalyzed by BT's Los Feliz move as well as his growing affinity for digital programs and virtual instruments (VSTs and DSPs—Digital Signal Processing instruments), has taken quite a while, but it's gradually becoming a workaday reality. BT expands upon his recent shift toward recording and creating in an almost all-digital, all-virtual instrument world: "In the early days, when I had my first touch of success, I went through this massive gear-surplus arc. I thought if only I had the latest 'insert gear name here,' I would be set. It got to the point where everything in my studio became Spinal Tap-ish. I was able to say, 'This is my 1967 badibaba,' but I used it only twice a year, if that."

BT'S DIGI TURNING POINT

"My biggest turning point was in 1994, when I got on a Macintosh and started to use the new Pro Tools software. I found that even during those early years the concept of plug-ins made so much sense to me—and even more so now. I'll be talking about that turning point my whole life."

A defining factor in BT deciding to scale back his new room was his awareness that he was using some of his vintage gear only for its name, and not on a consistent basis. Even with his amazing catalog of gear—including beautiful, classic pieces such as the Arp 2600, old Moogs, Roland modulators, the list goes on—BT often found himself amidst a pile of manuals with nothing actually constructive taking place. "I realized that having so much gear was distracting me from the process of making music. I would spend most of my time deciding on the best piece of gear to use in a certain song, and I would spend hours on end making sure I was getting the exact sound I wanted. No real creating was going on." Spending days building a signal chain or extracting a sound from a piece of gear became too time-consuming. BT took a step back and realized that the virtual recording world he had been toying with might be a better tool for the style of music he was producing and creating.

BT's transition from analog tracking to digital recording didn't necessarily mean

Hard drives and outboard gear in BT's upstairs entryway.

he had to leave those old sounds behind. By experimenting with Pro Tools as well as other systems including Logic Audio, Massive, Nuendo, and Acid, BT has furthered the art of reproducing his familiar old sounds with new cutting-edge tools. BT's latest toy is Kyma, "an extremely powerful synthesis and sound-design tool for constructing sounds from the ground up."

BT explains how the new digital programs emulate analog's thick, warm tones by computing and reproducing an almost perfect analog sound wave. "The thing is, sound is actually a quantifiable thing. Analog gear exerts a specific effect on audio material. With digital sound, programmers and sound engineers have studied how the analog sound waves react, and they make this into an algorithm. They then use that algorithm for the digital programs. For example, if they want to understand how sound is acting when, say, a cymbal runs through a UREI 1176 compressor, they are able to study and quantify the harmonics, do a few more things, and then make that into an algorithm. Understanding what sound engineers do when programming helps me know how to use the digital recording tools and make it sound the way I want it to."

BT goes even further by stating that as engineers study sound and perfect how it reacts in a digital medium, analog at some point will be antiquated. Digital's ability to reproduce analog sounds to near perfection may not sway analog purists—for whom analog will always be far superior to digital—but in BT's mind, it is idyllic. "The thing that excites me is the ease with which you can get through your own creative personal barriers to get to the final outcome. Actualizing it in real time is an amazing thing. For many musicians, getting the idea out fast is sometimes the only

BT's DAW workspace—clean, clear, no clutter.

way you can really hear what your ear wants to hear. To me, when you impede that process, the actual sound you imagined fades away."

Of course, being fast doesn't necessarily mean being better. BT recognizes that not everything can be done on a computer, and there are times when "real" sounds and Old School tools are necessary. "Nothing replaces using a nice Neve module or a great ADR tube compressor, and nothing will ever compare to hearing a real orchestra versus a mocked-up orchestra programmed through virtual synths—but being able to sit down and actualize a sound in Giga Sampler, instead of having to notate each instrument, is extremely helpful. When I want to mock up an orchestral arrangement, I can do it fairly fast. I can know exactly where the inner voice is supposed to go and then hear how it sounds almost instantaneously—as opposed to in the past, where a composer like Debussy sat at the piano and composed each voice. Even just a few years ago, scoring took a much longer time. The barriers are dropping, which is thrilling."

The skeptics of immediate composition may not quite understand BT's enthusiasm for digital recording, but BT explains away the skepticism. "It's funny: I remember seven years ago thinking that if I bought something and didn't have an object to hold, it felt odd. I couldn't handle that a program could live only in my computer." As BT's use of plug-ins accelerated and the virtual programs' interfaces became more aesthetically pleasing, BT made a mental leap. "It got to where I would open up a new piece of software and think, Wow—here is my new synth! For whatever reason, at that point I realized there wasn't any difference—a synthesizer is actually a computer. It has a CPU [central processing unit], it runs on an operating system, it has all of the same stuff. The only difference is the program that was running on a synthesizer is now running on a host computer. At that point I became conscious to the fact that

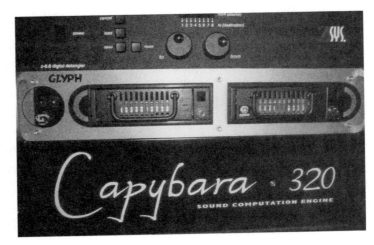

A ZSys digital patch bay and Glyph carriage with removable hard drives atop a Capybara 320 multi-processing, synthesis, and sample processor for Kyma.

sitting behind a keyboard is no different from sitting behind a computer. I am playing the same notations or sounds, just on a different medium. It doesn't make virtual synths and plug-ins any less valid." As for immediacy affecting sound quality, BT continues, "I am actually getting better sounds. That is the most exciting thing: The sounds you can make with the new plug-ins are so much more cutting-edge than anything you can get from a keyboard and running it through effects." Now, instead of buying expensive vintage or state-of-the-art gear, BT goes online to find shareware, freeware, plug-ins, and much more. "People from around the world are writing these amazing synth/edit coding programs. Some of this stuff, as well as the programs you can buy,

---

ELECTRONICA'S INITIATIVE

"Electronica and punk have a definite similarity: They both totally prescribe to a DIY aesthetic. We both tried to work within the constructs of the traditional music business, but the system didn't get us—so we found a way to do it for ourselves, before it became affordable." —BT

---

are phenomenal." BT's discoveries run the gamut from offbeat programs that only the most devoted techno-geek can find to prototypical programs such as Reaktor (a kind of toolkit for musicians to build their own modified virtual synthesizers), Absynth (another modifiable program to create virtual synthesizers), and FM7 (a desktop program for reading and emulating original FM synths). These allow for almost all of BT's previous "hard" keyboards to live virtually in his computers. Today BT is finding that his virtual instruments and plug-ins are often more powerful and more exhilarating than many of the keyboards out on the market. "If you were to sit down on a keyboard at a Guitar Center, and that keyboard was able to play some of the sounds I am getting with these programs, you would go crazy. You would sell your car to buy some of those sounds."

The instant gratification allowed by BT's approach is not for every musician, and the immediacy of such tools can be dangerous. By allowing artists to speed up the learning curve of recording, technology can replace having to learn important fundamentals. Many musicians are now oblivious as to how to play a piano, guitar, or violin, or even set up a simple mic chain. An understanding of the basic principles of playing instruments and the intricacies of gear can now be replaced with easy-to-get plug-ins. BT warns, "There are people who will use technology for the wrong thing. They try to get things done fast without understanding the principles behind music and recording. Musicians can't learn anything if they just sit in front of a computer. They are missing the point of music, which is to make things sound beautiful, harsh,

(Top) BT's Line 6 guitar amp; (bottom) Access Virus Indigo analog modeling synthesizer and Apple laptop.

or whatever. If they lose their musicianship, then the sounds will lose their personality. Artists should need to cathartically purge themselves. If they only think technically, they will not connect with people emotionally. Artists need to understand both sides."

The luxury and flexibility digital technology offers is revolutionizing the recording industry. If that flexibility can be leveraged while keeping musicianship and creativity intact, many more musicians may want to try BT's mode of going home, lighting a candle, turning on a computer, and making music. BT summarizes his electronic vision: "I think everyone is going to move in this digital direction. Whether you are in the electronic-music genre or whether you are a rock band, the ability to do nonlinear recording is remarkable and should not be passed up. I am ready for the Tera Computer, where I can have two laptops, sit in Thailand, and make records. That is where I'm at."

TECH TALK
Acronyms For Virtual Instruments

VSTi: Virtual Studio Technology instrument. Created by Steinberg Instruments, this standard can run in any VST 2.0-compatible host (including Logic and Cubase).

DirectConnect: A standard created by Digidesign for use with Pro Tools or another TDM-compatible host.

MAS: A standard created by Mark Of The Unicorn for use with its program Digital Performer.

DirectX: The Microsoft standard used by such programs as Cakewalk Sonar.

Creating A Digital Audio Workstation

Creating a DAW doesn't have to be complex.

1. Buy a PC or Mac with a sound card and plenty of hard-drive space.

2. Install whatever software is appropriate, such as Logic or Digital Performer. Pro Tools can also do some sequencing, but it is used mainly for editing.

3. Buy a mic, plug it in, and begin to experiment.

"The barriers that impede the creative process are just dropping, which is so exciting." —BT

BT multiprocesses with his two Apple Titanium laptops.

BT ON SONGWRITING

"I sing my song idea in my head for a couple of days. Almost a hundred times out of a hundred, I go to a piano or an acoustic guitar and record the idea onto a little cassette; then I listen to it and think about how I can make it interesting. I have to hear the melody first—there has to be something there that's dramatic and inspires me to actually sit down on an instrument and try to write a good piece of music. Once I get that feeling, that theme, that idea, I try to augment it with cutting-edge technology. That is the process for me."

BT On His First Studio

"When I was recording my first record, I was still working from my bedroom, using very basic pieces of gear. I had a TVC 386 [an Intel processor for PCs, fast then but considered slow now], a Boss 8-channel mixer with no midrange EQ, an Akai MPC60, a Roland D-70, and a Korg O3R DAT. That was it—a lot of equipment, I guess, but old and slow by today's standards. I just did a lecture at the University of Berkeley, California—my alma mater—and I saw all of their new synth workstations. They have ten times the equipment I had to make my first album, but all in one single synth workstation. Amazing!"

One of BT's guitars hangs on the wall of his workspace.

BT's Current Studio Setup

BT's studio is stripped down and digi-basic. When he performs live, he is known to work off nothing more than a pair of Apple Titanium laptops and some software. His home studio setup is equally elegant but a bit more powerful. "I have two computers: a Mac and a PC. My Mac is running Logic Audio and Pro Tools, and the PC is running Giga, Reaktor, and Acid. I also have a VSTi host. So the basics of my studio are the plug-ins that live in my very powerful computers. I have about 500 VSTi instruments, and I have made hundreds of sounds for them. Each one of those sampled instruments is, in fact, a powerful synthesizer in its own right."

BT's Real-Time Woes

"One of my favorite things about today's technology is that we can get so intricate with timing. In a performance we are able to stack a lot more stuff and it doesn't feel messy—but in doing this, it's important to allot enough room for each piece of sonic information. My songs are very multi-textural and multi-layered; sometimes there are hundreds if not thousands of hours of work in a song. There are songs that I put six weeks into just to be in perfect time, which is an incredibly tedious process down to every 64th-note. That also includes making sure everything but the kick drum and bass are shelved at 100Hz–120Hz, cutting out the bottom end. This allows all the other instruments—which sometimes clutter the mix with sub-harmonic information—to be contained, so only the kick drum and bass line move the speaker diaphragms. The result is clarity in the mix; each piece has its own little place in the song's universe. This analytical part is exciting for me, because things can be made really dense, complex, and interesting. Ultimately it is important to create a song that can reach the listeners, so that even though it may be complex, it feels very simple. To balance the analytical process with the creative process, that is what I strive for—marrying great traditional songwriting with cutting-edge technology."

BT's 5.1 Concept

"I have been doing more film scores [*Go, The Fast and the Furious, Monster*, etc.] and working a lot in 5.1, so I decided to put a 5.1 setup in my new studio, which is awesome. I am really experimenting with it. Instead of the lame way most people mix in 5.1, where they put the strings in the front and the string ambience in the back, I am more like, 'What if you do it in a Debussy style and split the violins front to back?' I am still working with that concept, though, and just playing around with it to see what works."

BASIC DIGITAL ACRONYMS

A/D: Analog-to-digital converter, a device that converts an analog signal into digital data.

ASCII: American Standard Code for Information Interchange, the standard set of 7-bit codes used to represent the keys on a computer keyboard.

BNC: A high-quality locking connector for two-conductor low-voltage electrical use.

CPU: Central processing unit, the main component of a computer's microprocessor.

DAE: Digidesign Audio Engine, a Macintosh application that puts the audio data on, and reads the data off, the hard disk. It can be run behind other applications such as Pro Tools.

DAW: Digital audio workstation, a computer or a stand-alone console with A/D and D/A converters. It has a high-capacity hard disk drive and software tools for recording, editing, and mixing.

DSP: Digital signal processing, a process of modifying audio in digital form.

MDM: Modular digital multitrack, a multitrack digital recorder that uses tape cartridges as a medium, such as the Alesis ADAT or the Tascam DA-88.

PCM: Pulse code modulation, a digital scheme for transmitting analog data. The signals in PCM are binary; that is, there are only two possible states, represented by logic 1 (high) and logic 0 (low). This is true no matter how complex the analog waveform happens to be. Using PCM, it is possible to digitize all forms of analog data, including full-motion video, voices, music, telemetry, and virtual reality (VR).

A Pro Tools rack complete with a couple of 888 and 1622 interfaces.

5.1 mixing: 5.1 mixing began (and is still normally used) for film scoring, to use audio perception to immerse the viewer/listener in the movie experience, and to take advantage of theater sound systems. In film, most of the sounds are placed in the front speakers, with just the ambient room sound in the rear speakers. There also may be some sound effects and room tones in the rears, but the perspective is still supposed to be from the middle of the screen.

Surround 5.1 is relatively new in the world of music mixing. Many engineers are trying to get hold of the concept of surround mixing but are floundering because there are no rules yet, and the electronic standards are still in flux. In addition, many engineers are grappling with perspective, e.g.: Do people want to hear singers behind them? Most people are still playing around with the concept of surround-sound in audio-only applications, so the rear speakers are often just an afterthought.

5.1 basics: 5.1 uses three speakers—left, right, and center—in front, plus two speakers in back, placed at a 110-degree angle. There is also a subwoofer, which represents the ".1" in 5.1. The sound can be panned to any of the speakers. Often the biggest change for an engineer in 5.1 is working with the center speaker. In stereo, a mixer/engineer might pan a sound to the middle by assigning it equally to the left and right speakers. Now, engineers working in 5.1 tend to put that same sound in the center speaker. This is a holdover from film, where the idea is to keep the viewer's attention on the middle of the screen. If dialogue is placed in the left or right speaker (or both), to people in aisle seats, the dialogue would seem to come from the closest speaker, not from the screen image. With film, putting the vocal in the middle

---

BT ON TURNTABLES:

"Turntables can be used as a primary instrument. The Invisibl Skratch Piklz—those guys are amazing. Turntables require an incredible amount of percussion technique, which is not widely recognized. In a way turntablism and scratch turntables are more complicated than traditional percussion instruments because they involve pitch and rhythm. It takes extraordinary dexterity and impeccable proficiency to play turntables."

speaker makes the sound seem like it is coming from the image, but this is not necessarily the best approach for mixing music in 5.1.

"Whatever your instrument is—piano, guitar, drums—learn your craft and instrument first. Then learn how to use the computer." —BT

Native Instruments: The following are examples of software instruments that can be played in realtime through MIDI keyboards and controllers. The software integrates with most audio/MIDI sequencers. The Native Instrument programs are compatible with most interface and plug–in formats made by other companies. They run on Mac or PCs.

- Pro-53
- Reaktor
- Absynth
- Ni-Spektral
- Battery

BT and DJing: "My DJing has totally changed. I have gone completely off my vinyl and am now using two Titanium laptops and two Oxygen 8's. I might play a song like the Beatles' 'Day Tripper' on top of Missy Elliott, or I might use something like Kraftwerk as a rhythmic background. Basically I have three tracks playing at once, which I could never do with turntables. Instead of beat-mixing in another track, I sit there with my headphones on, copy-read them, and write an Acid line in key with everything I am playing. It's simple—I am writing music live and beat-mixing in the Acid line. I then beat-mix in the breakbeat and start pulling out the original track so I don't have too many sounds in the mix. I am writing and reading all at once—creating a new track that never existed before—on the spot. Sometimes people come up to ask where they can get the track, and I'm like, 'You can't.'"

Chapter Four

311

North Hollywood, California

"Good rock played live will never go away."

311'S SOUND IS A HYBRID of alternative rock fundamentals mixed with reggae riffs, funky rhythms, and dueling voices which create a melodious rap/vocal interplay. This fusion—a distinctive trademark of the band since its early-'90s inception—has become a staple of the alt-rock genre at large, and its elements have infused practically every popular music style. But for whatever reason, many musicians and critics alike neglect or do not understand 311's seminal role in the art of genre-blending. No matter: 311 remains steadfast, vigilantly continuing to cultivate their craft and career. 311 is a case study in band perseverance, and the Hive—the studio named after the group's large and

311's live room, with (left to right) Nick Hexum, P-Nut (in the background), Chad Sexton on drums, and SA Martinez.

extremely dedicated fan club—is central to 311's perseverance, as its acquisition and renovation symbolizes and solidifies their dedication to each other and their music.

The members of 311 (Tim Mahoney, Nick Hexum, P-Nut, SA Martinez, and Chad Sexton) have plunked themselves and the Hive in the heart of the North Hollywood warehouse district, a place where musicians struggle for hours on end to rehearse and record in C-level through A-level studios. In a roundabout way, the Hive's locale can be seen as a reminder for up-and-coming L.A. musicians that maintaining a music-industry career means more than just landing a record contract, and much more than simply wanting to be rich and famous. 311 have sold over 7 million albums in the U.S. and have toured successfully for more than 12 years. As a result, the band members have made a good chunk of money from their music, but rather than spending it on opulent lifestyles, they've invested much of their earnings into the Hive, and they continue to reap the rewards of their musical returns.

311's commitment to their art is evident from the surroundings in the Hive. Numerous cargo rigs and crates with the 311 insignia are scattered about, a hint that the band is about to embark on yet another leg of what seems like a never-ending touring schedule. Mounds of guitar gear, such as Tim's Bad Cat and Mesa/Boogie & Bogner amps, are stacked in his section of the live room. Adjacent to Tim's alcove is P-Nut's nook, complete with an upright bass. Nick and SA's lyric books and sheets sit atop a few Old School black metal music stands, and Chad's kit is tucked in the back of the room, complete with stacks and stacks of drumsticks. Lead singer Nick Hexum and drummer Chad Sexton—the band's self-appointed studio devotees—give some insight into the Hive and why it is so important when it comes to perfecting their craft.

Cargo rigs and touring crates with 311's trademark insignia on the Hive's outside patio.

"We started out recording in my dad's basement—with just a pool table and a 4-track recorder." —Nick Hexum

"We have learned the basics of recording on our own and have accumulated pieces of gear over time—but once we took on the Hive, it was another whole level," says Nick. It allowed the bandmembers to satisfy their technical curiosity and learn the formal aspects of engineering, in turn helping them cultivate their overall sound. Nick continues, "We have to give a huge thanks to our producer, Ron Saint Germain, because he was kind of like our engineering dad. He wanted to show us the ropes—helping to choose the board, redesigning portions of the rooms. He went all out for us and is an all-around amazing producer." Besides helping 311 with engineering techniques, Ron gave them tips on buying gear. He even phoned up friends and went on eBay to get the best pieces of equipment in good condition and at good prices. Chad elaborates a bit more on Ron Saint Germain's influence: "Saint deserves all of the credit. He got us started on learning about mic positioning, phase relationships, and all of that good stuff." Inspired by Ron, Chad has stepped up his efforts to study the science of acoustics and its role in recording. Nick explains Chad's new love for engi-

Guitarist Tim Mahoney.

neering: "Chad is a student of the art. He knows what he's doing—not just when it comes to drum sounds, but also with mixing and live miking. I love how Saint always gives us a new perspective, but Chad can do it now as well. Sometimes Chad is even pickier than Saint!" Whatever the situation, 311 finds how to control things and make it work for them, and such is the case with their studio.

311 had to revamp the Hive (formerly known as Chateau Studios) to make sure the facility stayed up to modern standards, but they also took the opportunity to transform the place to fit their recording style. First they had to perform some basic modifications. The floor had been torn apart, likely an aftereffect from when the former occupants took out all of the cabling. 311 asked Saint, Todd Smith, and Tommy Hillman to help rebuild the whole room. Chad explains, "It took a good three months. The floor had this messed-up configuration, so we had to set down a solid floor foundation." Nick elaborates on the floor's renovation. "There was this huge trough, which they filled up with sand and cement. They also flattened out this weird dip in the back." The floor in the live room is now up to par, with a great sound.

After dealing with the live room, 311 researched what board would work best for their tight but raucous performances. They were looking for a console with the warm sound of older analog boards, but they also wanted state-of-the-art automation. "We always said that if we could ever get a Neve, we would," says Nick. "Neves sound so amazing. But we just kind of figured that the older Neves were out of our reach. We've also used digital boards like the Yamaha O2R for pre-production and loved its 'recalla-

Chad Sexton pulls up a few mixes on the AMEK 72-input 9098i board.

bility.' So we were looking for a board that had both great sound and great automation." With Saint's guidance, 311 began to research the AMEK 72-input 9098i designed by the world-renowned Rupert Neve, who was responsible for creating the indispensable old Neve analog boards. "The AMEK ended up being almost exactly what we were looking for," says Nick. "It's a really good analog board, but you can recall and control everything digitally." Chad adds, "The AMEK is essentially a Neve, but it obviously has different configurations and, more important, a vertical patch bay—which means everyone has to relearn a few things." That takes time and energy, two things most producers and engineers don't have.

"I sent our new material that we recorded on the AMEK to our mastering guy, Joe Gastworth. He has worked with everyone: NoFX, the Beach Boys, the Grateful Dead, you name it. He called me freaking out, saying, 'I don't like modern music, but I love this shit!'" —Chad Sexton

When looking for a board, most audiophiles ask for an SSL for its ease of use, or an old Neve console for its warm sound. The "newness" of the AMEK did not scare off 311. They were already in the midst of learning the intricacies of other high-end recording systems—consoles, outboard gear, and the like—so learning the fine points of one more board did not matter. "We never really knew the full ins and outs of boards, except for a few digital models," Chad continues. "So in a way we were starting from scratch on the AMEK, and that made it easier for us to learn the board's

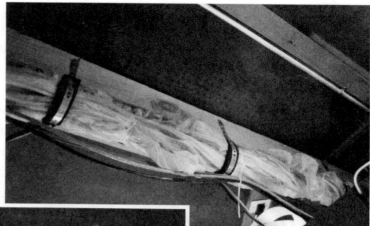

(Top) Cabling runs to guitar amps isolated upstairs. (Left) 311's Studer A-827 24-track machine.

details. Basically our minds were open to almost everything." Nick interrupts, "But Chad is the one really going all out in the learning process. The rest of us are just kind of learning the board's basics." Although the AMEK is not generally sought out by audio aficionados, its availability and great sound make it a perfect board for a band like 311.

Overall, the Hive has been customized to capture the raw essence of 311's live shows while maintaining the sonic precision of a high-tech studio—to bridge the gap between a studio recording's sterility and the unholy feedback of a live show. That balance can be hard to attain. "One of the charms of working on analog gear is that it leaves in more personality," comments Nick. "If we relied too much on digital, we'd be naturally inclined to move things around to make more of a slick product." 311 has also tried changing the rooms' logistics to track live. Nick continues, "We like to track live but without atmosphere noise. Normally we put all of our guitar cabinets in iso booths to prevent bleeding, but since our space was limited, we decided to use an empty room upstairs to house the amps. We ran all of our mic and speaker cables to the cabinets upstairs. Now we can all play and track at once to get that live vibe, without the extreme ambient noise." At first 311 worried that the sounds from the upstairs room would be clinical or contrived, but as Nick puts it, "We feel that we are getting some of the best sounds we've ever gotten, and that is what matters." Still, Nick points out that having a dialed-in live-room setup doesn't mean there isn't room for tweaking. "We are still constantly adjusting the sounds. The room's dynamics keep changing—the liveness, the positioning, all of that—but in the end, tracking live helps us maintain that raw sound."

REDUCTION IN BOARD PRICE:

"We were able to get the AMEK at a fairly inexpensive price—our board came from R. Kelly's old studio." —Nick Hexum

---

The refurbished Hive has brought 311 into a new realm of experimentation in perfecting sound while understanding acoustics and sound dynamics at a more professional level. Nick adds his perspective: "We've learned that overall we want a crisp yet warm sound, which we get with the AMEK. We don't like to have to muddle with too many effects." Chad adds, "I think people can tell our songs are full performances, not just the clip-and-clip of editing through Pro Tools." While not opposed to digital editing, 311 wants to avoid getting to the point where entire songs are clipped *ad nauseam*. "Some people want drums to be perfect, so they cut up the live drums to match a perfect grid," says Nick. "We might take a drum loop and move it a bit to match up with the live drumming. We basically wrap the loops around everything else so it has more of a live, natural, human feel. So we have a slightly different, imperfect approach."

Diving into sound engineering has given 311 a more precise ear, one that can differentiate between subtleties they once ignored. "You have to know what you are doing when you are recording digitally," says Chad. "Getting hot levels on digital is a complete mistake. Even at home on my Digi 001, a cheap Pro Tools card, if I keep pushing a sound past the normal level, I hear brittleness, like a 'tzzzz.' The sound just fractures. I can hear the squareness of the wave topping out." Chad adds another esoteric theory to his digital recording approach: "I get worried when the highs start to cut off, because I think all of the imaging is up there around 100kHz. Basically our ears stop hearing at about 20k, and most Neve boards go up to about 40k. The AMEK board responds to around 110k, so it's still getting that high end. I think in that range, people hear something subconsciously. When we're playing or recording, I think we have this connection around 100k; it's there, but we can't hear it. It's a hippie kind of theory. But hey, it follows similar theories, you know, where scientists proclaim that all atoms are connected by a string." Chad's high-frequency theory may be a bit esoteric, but it works for the band. Nick adds, "Whatever it is, we definitely have this subconscious feeling when recording, vibing off each other. It's kind of like when you're taking a hearing test. You can't say, Okay—now it's on or off. It's like messing with the other sound waves."

For 311, the Hive is a training ground for learning all the theories and techniques of recording music—esoteric or otherwise. The band's love for making music, combined with their ardent drive and solidarity, has allowed them to keep their grassroots fan base and fulfill a lifelong dream with the Hive: to evolve and cultivate their craft and career on their own terms. "We don't listen to what other people say," says Nick. "We are really strong-willed about what we are going to do. We've always made it about us and our music. We try to be just a classic rock band with a great natural vibe. I think what we have achieved is more of a timeless sound."

Tim in the Hive's entryway.

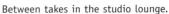
Between takes in the studio lounge.

TECH TALK
Microphone Basics

Microphones are transducers that change sound waves into electrical signals. A mic is often the first piece of gear in a recording chain, and each mic has a unique sound quality and characteristic.

The classification of a mic depends on how it converts acoustic energy into electrical voltages. *Dynamic mics* have membranes that move within a magnetic field. These membranes (or *diaphragms*) move slightly when sound hits them, creating a small electric current. Dynamic microphones come in two varieties:

Moving coil: This variety uses a magnet and a coil wrapped with wire. When the sound pressure hits the diaphragm, the coil moves across the magnetic field.

Ribbon: These use very thin strips of metal (sometimes gold) that also operate in a magnetic field. Ribbon mics are usually rectangle-shaped, have a very low output, and have a softer, non-grating high end good for brass or drum overheads, and sometimes vocals. They can distort more easily than other types of microphones.

An AKG C-12 VR placed as an overhead mic.

Condenser microphones use thin metal diaphragms, flat and back-to-back, with an electrical current running between them. When sound hits the metal, the current changes, which is extrapolated as sound. Most of these mics need 48 volts of phantom power to operate. Condensers usually sound brighter and can track high frequencies more accurately than dynamic microphones. Tube mics are condenser mics that have tube power supplies, so they don't need phantom power, and the sound is amplified through its own tube circuit, which warms the sound. Some condenser mics come with a –10dB pad.

Mic patterns: A microphone's pattern refers to its directional response—how it picks up sounds from different directions. Sounds coming into the front of the mic are said to be *on axis*; all other directions are called *off axis*.

Cardioid or unidirectional mics (for example, the Shure SM57) are most sensitive to sound coming from directly in front. Sounds coming from the rear and side end up being lower in volume than on-axis sounds.

Hyper-cardioid mics (for example, the Audio-Technica ATM41HE) are similar to cardioids, but with an even narrower pattern: Sounds coming from behind are picked up even less by this kind of mic.

Figure-8 or bi-directional mics (for example, the RCA 44) pick up sounds on either side but are least sensitive to sounds that are 90 degrees off-axis.

Omnidirectional mics pick up sounds evenly, with an even frequency response, from all directions.

Some mics, such as the AKG C-414, have a switch that allows you to change the pattern. Others do not; for instance, the RCA 44 is a figure-8-pattern mic only.

Mic Preamps

Mic preamps (or mic pre's) can be outboard, such as the Neve 1073, or included in the mixing console. (Outboard mic pre's tend to be a bit better in quality.) Mic signals are very weak, so it's necessary to boost the signal to line level so it can be used by the console. A mic preamp sometimes comes with a pad. A pad is simply a few resistors that cut the level going into the mic pre. If the pad button is punched, it reduces the volume (usually by −10dB), which is needed if the circuit is distorting.

The Console

Major manufacturers of mixing boards include Trident, Neve, Mackie, Helios, SSL, and AMEK. A console allows an engineer to take mic- or line-level signals, blend in effects, shape the sounds, mix them together, and record them onto tape or disk, and also to create monitor mixes for the musicians who are tracking. A console can also be used solely for monitoring. Here are a few basic console-flow principles.

Understanding console signal flow:

1. A mic signal must first be boosted by a mic preamp (either in the board or outboard). Once the signal is at line level, it can be recorded and/or monitored.

2. The signal now goes to a multitrack tape machine or to a digital recording system such as Pro Tools. One possible path is for the signal to be assigned to travel through the channel's fader to a *bus*. A bus is a common signal line; it can comprise one signal or a number of blended signals. The bus delivers the signal to the tape machine at a certain level, which is set by a fader for that bus.

3. The signal can be routed back to the console again through a line input and into another channel (now called a monitoring channel). At this point, the signal is sent internally to the board's stereo bus to be monitored. The signals returning to the board (perhaps from different tracks on tape) can now be sent to both the studio's monitor speakers and a 2-track recorder, which can be another analog tape machine, another couple of Pro Tools tracks, or even a cassette deck.

So, the general signal chain is as follows: Mic input, to channel fader, to assigned bus, to multitrack recorder, to monitoring channel, to the stereo bus and stereo bus master fader, to the monitor speakers and 2-track recorder.

Console designs: In a *split console*, there is one path for each I/O (channel). Basically, the signal travels into the channel and then goes to the multitrack or monitors. In an *in-line console* (311's AMEK has in-line architecture), each I/O has two

The Hive's Studio Gear

AMEK 9098i Rupert Neve 72-input console
Pro Tools 192 HD (2)
Pro Tools Sync
Pro Tools MIDI Time
Pro Tools 80GB HD (5)
Studer A827
Otari MTR 90
Eventide H3000D/SX
T.C. Electronic D-two
Lexicon Super PrimeTime Digital Delay
Lexicon 200 digital reverb
Effectron 2
dbx 120XP Subharmonic Synth
Summit Audio EQF-100 (2)
Tube Tech PE-1C
Avalon 737sp mic pre (2)
Empirical Labs Distressor EL8-X (2)
Universal Audio 1176N blackface (2)
Universal Audio/UREI LA-4 blackface
dbx 160SL stereo compressor/limiter
Alesis Masterlink ML9600 hard-disk recorder
Apogee PSX100 24-bit A-D/D-A converter
Little Labs AES digital audio router
HHB CDR 85 CD-R recorder
Timeline/Micro Lynx
Rosendahl Nanosyncs reference generator
Brainstorm Dual Timecode Distributor/Reshaper
Byston 4B amp (2)
Tannoy 1200 monitors
Pro Acc CC2 monitors
Mics:
AKG C-451B (6)
AKG C-12
AKG C-414B/ULS
AKG C-1000S (2)
Beyerdynamic M160 (2)
Coles 87 (2)
Crown PZM 30D (2)
Electro-Voice RE-20
Neumann KM184 (2)
Neumann M149
Sennheiser MD421 (4)
Sennheiser MD441U
Shure SM7
Shure SM57
Shure SM69
Shure SM91

separate input and output paths, or two faders. One fader can go to the multitrack, while the other fader can be used to listen to the signal coming from the multitrack. One could be set for tape monitoring, while the other could then be set for the mix. Most in-line consoles have a button that allows the engineer to assign either fader to either job.

Faders and their roles: Each channel fader takes in a line- or mic-level signal and sends it to the multitrack tape machine. This is accomplished with a direct patch or by using the multitrack busses.

The stereo bus master fader is one stereo or two mono faders that control the level of the stereo bus. The

Chad Sexton and 311's studio engineer Zack Barnhorst check to see if the faders work.

stereo bus is where the channel signals come together and are sent to tape; the monitoring bus goes to the speakers. Sometimes this is the same signal, but one fader controls the volume coming out of the control room monitors, and the other controls the level going onto tape.

Each monitor fader receives a line input from the multitrack tape recorder. The job you give the fader—e.g., guitar, bass, vocal 1, etc.—determines the fader's name for the rest of the mixing process.

"Rupert Neve actually stopped by the Hive to see our AMEK. He walked into the control room and began moving his hand about two inches over the board. He stopped at one spot and said, 'There is one fan out.' Sure enough, a fan was disconnected in the back. So he reached around and plugged it in. It was amazing." —Chad Sexton

---

Patch Bay Basics

The *patch bay* is a system of panel-mounted connectors that form groups of inputs and outputs. They are routed with plug-in patch cords. The patch bay allows an engineer to connect gear in an easy manner without having to crawl behind the console.

A typical horizontal patch bay is built with two rows stacked on top of each other. Ordinarily the top row is for outputs and the bottom row is for inputs, although each patch bay setup is tailor-made to fit the studio.

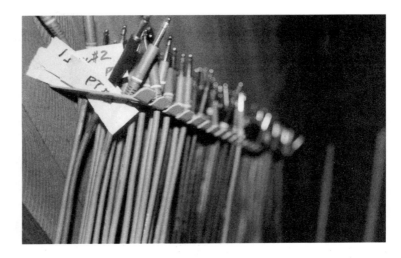

A bundle of TT patch cables.

(311's AMEK uses a less common vertical patch bay, which is set up a bit differently.)

When nothing is plugged into the patch bay, the hard-wired gear functions normally. For example, a keyboard might be hard-wired through the patch bay to go to a certain console channel. But if the engineer wants the keyboard to go to a different channel, he can do this simply by inserting a patch cord into the patch bay—there is no need to rewire the synth. This simplifies studio wiring and rerouting.

A room view with Nick's hard-wired keyboard and SA's turntables.

Normaling: If a patch cable is plugged into any input or output, the signal path is broken. This is called *full normaling*—the patch bay connection remains intact until another piece of gear is plugged in. In *half normaling*, the signal path is uninterrupted when a piece of gear is plugged in, allowing the engineer to split and redirect the signal somewhere else, similar to what can be done with a Y connector.

Patch bay types: There are a few fundamentally different types of patch bays. Smaller studios and home installations often use economical "home-grade" patch bays (they normally cost about $100) fitted with ¼" jacks for ¼" unbalanced plugs. These patch bays can use standard guitar cables for connections, but runs should be no more than 20 feet long—unbalanced cables longer than 20 feet can degrade high-end frequencies and may also pick up a bit of hum. Balanced cables use three conductors and often have TRS (tip-ring-sleeve) plugs. Balanced cables can be used for runs up to 1,000 feet without significant sound degradation.

Studio-grade patch bays are not the same as less-expensive home patch bays. TRS connectors are needed for studio-grade patch bays. Both types use ¼" jacks—but unbalanced guitar-cable plugs don't fit precisely in these TRS jacks and will eventually spread a studio patch bay's jacks and ruin them. A studio tech will kill someone if he sees a guitar cable plugged into a TRS studio patch bay!

Many higher-end studios use patch bays fitted with smaller TT ("Tiny Telephone") connectors. TT cables offer optimal sound quality in a small size, allowing for a greater number of patch points in a small area compared to ¼" TRS plugs.

"I think we put two mics on the drums and crossed our fingers." —Chad Sexton

---

Mic Preamp Testing

Sometimes it's hard to figure out how the sound changes with a new mic preamp, or if it changes at all. Here's a basic way to test out a new mic pre:

1. Listen to a mic like a Shure SM58 (or any mic, really) through the existing chain.

2. Plug the same mic into the new preamp—which is now sending a line level to the mixer—and then plug it back into the existing preamp and compare and contrast the sound.

3. Try different sources—guitar, male vocal, female vocal, piano, etc. Continue to test and make notes of how the sounds change—it's all about comparing and contrasting.

Mastering Programs

Musicians recording digitally can benefit from the good home mastering programs/plug-ins available, such as T-RackS 24 Stand-alone Analog Mastering Suite for

SA and Nick tracking in the live room.

Mac/PC. It allows musicians to master their own mixes on the desktop. (Of course, such a program will not replace a good mastering engineer.) T-RackS 24 includes: a 6-band mastering EQ, tube-modeled stereo compressor, multi-band master limiter, soft-clipping output stage, and studio mastering presets.

The Hive's Solid Floor

The Hive's rebuilt floor is solid and "floated," or mechanically isolated from the rest of the building. If a studio floor is not solid or floated, noise can travel through the mic stands and into the mics.

Drum loops: A drum loop is a few bars of a drum performance that is pasted over and over again, so that it loops. It's possible to build an entire song out of four or five loops.

(Clockwise from top left) SA's music stand; Tim's Furman headphone mixer; Chad's pile of Zildjian sticks; pedals and a head stack including a Bad Cat, Mesa/Boogie, and Bogner.

311's Gear

Nick Hexum's guitars include: Gibson Les Paul, Ovation acoustic/electric, and Martin acoustic. His amp is a Rivera Bonehead with a 4x12 cabinet and 2x12 sub-woofer. Nick uses Seymour Duncan pickups. His non-guitar gear includes: Macintosh G4, Nord Lead keyboard, Akai S-3000, Roland JV2080, Waldorf Pulse. He uses Pro Tools, Unity Session, Sample Tank, Battery, Echo Farm, and Amplitude software.

Tim Mahoney's guitars include: Paul Reed Smith Standard 24 (light blue, all mahogany, with a Bob Vessells custom tiki-mask inlay on the headstock), PRS Santana, PRS Custom 24 (mahogany w/maple top), PRS McCarty archtop, PRS

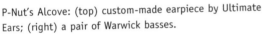

P-Nut's Alcove: (top) custom-made earpiece by Ultimate
Ears; (right) a pair of Warwick basses.

Standard (all mahogany), Schecter C7+ 7-string, and Washburn Dimebag Darrell
Signature Model. His amps include: Mesa/Boogie Triple Rectifier, Bogner Ubershall,
and Bad Cat Hot Cat Fender Twin Reverb, with Mesa/Boogie and Bogner speaker
cabinets. Effects include: Boss Octave; Electro-Harmonix Small Stone Phaser, Q-Tron,
Memory Man, Small Clone Chorus, Holy Grail Reverb, Mu-Tron 3 envelope filter,
Mu-Tron Phasor 2, Fulltone overdrive, Buda Wah and Dimebag Wah pedals, Rocktron
Intellifex, Lexicon PCM 42 digital delay, Line 6 DL4, and Boomerang Phase Sampler.
Tim uses Seymour Duncan pickups and Handycableable custom-fit cabling by
Handroll.

P-Nut's basses include: Warwick Streamer Stage II amber 5-string with afzelea
body, Warwick Streamer Stage II chocolate 5-string, Warwick Corvette bolt-on-neck 5-
string with bubinga body, fretless Warwick Thumb Bass bubinga 5-string, Warwick
Streamer maple 4-string, Warwick Alien acoustic bass, and '64 Fender Jazz Bass. His

Chad's maple-shell drum kit made by Orange County Drum and Percussion.

amps include SWR Bass 750 and SWR 800 power amps, and two 8x10 Megoliath speaker cabinets. P-Nut sometimes uses an Electro-Harmonix Big Muff pedal; his pickups are Basslines in a Jazz-style configuration.

SA Martinez uses Shure wireless mics, Rane mixers, and Technics turntables.

Chad Sexton's maple-shell drums are made by Orange County Drum & Percussion. His toms include: 7x8, 8x10, 10x12, 12x14, and 14x16. Chad uses Remo drum heads: clear Emperors on top, clear Ambassadors on bottom. His bass drum is a 18x 22 with reinforced shell, coated Power Stroke head on the beater side, black Power Stroke with hole on the front side. His snare is a 5½x14 or 6½x14, sometimes with a Falam head—both coated and clear (yellow), or sometimes a coated Emperor or Ambassador.

Chad's Zildjian cymbals include: "A" Custom 14" hi-hat, "K" 17" Custom dark crash, two "K" 20" Pre-Aged Dry Light Rides, "A" 22" Ping Ride Brilliant Finish, "A" 10" splash, and two "A" 18" Medium Thin Crashes. Specialty cymbals include: 20" Oriental series China, 12" and 10" Latin Azukas, and 8" and 10" Oriental Splashes.

Chad's hardware and pedals are made by Pearl. His pedals include Grip Peddler pads. He uses Zildjian sticks.

Chapter Five

System Of A Down's Daron Malakian
Glendale, California

"I am into skeletons and I like skulls. It's a good vibe for me."

BLENDING HARD-HITTING METAL WITH doses of melodic mysticism, syncopated thrash beats, and operatic vocal ferocity is not easy to pull off—yet in the late 1990s, System Of A Down bolted into the limelight with this enigmatic musical equation. System's guitarist, Daron Malakian, helped cultivate their musical formula by meshing metal virtuosity with pinches of subtonic classical phrasings, enough to suggest that Daron may have had a few classical guitar lessons or even a course or two in music theory. Yet despite the complexity of Daron's guitar parts, his personal approach to making music is deceptively simple. When producing and recording, he

Daron's Gear

Guitars & basses:
1968 Gibson ES-150, natural-finish hollowbody

1968 Gibson Firebird, sunburst

1971 Gibson Firebird, sunburst

Vintage '70s Gibson 4-string bass, brown

1978 Gibson Les Paul Custom, burgundy redburst

Early-'70s Gibson SG, burgundy

1970 Gibson SG, brown

1957 Gibson Les Paul Junior, sunburst

1980 ('58 reissue) Gibson Les Paul Heritage, gold/orange

2001 Gibson Les Paul Standard, black

1979 Gibson ES-347, black hollowbody

Early '70s Gibson Les Paul Custom, black

Ace Frehley signature series Gibson Les Paul

1978 Gibson Les Paul (custom shop), dark green

1977 Gibson Les Paul Custom, natural finish

Gibson ES-335, burgundy hollowbody

1969 Gibson Les Paul Custom, black

1973 Gibson Les Paul Custom, black

Gibson Doubleneck SG, white

Mid-'70s Gretsch with built-in phaser, grey

1978 Ibanez Iceman PS-10, cracked mirror

1979 Ibanez Iceman PS-10, black w/butterfly pickups

Ibanez Iceman, custom-made silver glitter

Ibanez Iceman, custom-made green/blue

(3) Ibanez Iceman, custom artwork by Vartan Malakian

(3) Ibanez Iceman 2, custom artwork by Vartan Malakian

Ibanez Iceman 2, hollowbody, custom artwork by Vartan Malakian

Ibanez Iceman, basic black

(2) Ibanez Iceman, custom-made baritone

Ibanez Artcore, AM73-TBL, blue

Ibanez Artcore, AG75-TBS, blue/black

Late-'90s Jackson Flying V, white

1966 Fender Jazzmaster, beige

Vintage Hagstrom, gold glitter sparkle

Martin GT-75, burgundy hollowbody

Martin 12-string acoustic guitar

Smith Guitar, Mel-O-Bar, stand-up slide, sunburst

GoldTone GT500 Banjitar

Norma Vegematic electric guitar

Yamaha APX-4A electric acoustic

Yamaha FG-400 acoustic

Applause AE-40 acoustic bass

Amps: Bad Cat 100-watt guitar head, Badcat 30-watt head, Bad Cat 30-watt combo amp, Traynor amp and cabinet, two Marshall ModeFour amp heads, two 1959 Watkins 15-watt Dominators, Ibanez Mini combo amp, Vox T-60 bass amp, Mini Marshall practice amp, and Carvin practice amp

Drums: Roland electronic five-piece V-Drums, Rogers vintage five-piece drum kit, Pacific five-piece drum kit, Tama four-piece drum kit, Tama steel snare drum, Remo doumbek, and custom-made Sako drums with iron snare

Keyboards: Korg 66-key keyboard, Kimball piano, Crate keyboard monitor system, Roland MC-909 drum machine/sampler, and Roland MC-505 drum machine.

Other studio gear: Mackie PA system with Yamaha speakers, JBL speakers with two JBL subwoofers, Roland monitor system, two Technics 1200 turntables, Pioneer turntable mixer with effects and samplers, two Pioneer CDJ1000s, and early-'80s Sharp dual cassette recorder

forgoes complicated tools and the physics of recording for a certain low-tech simplicity. Daron is a right-side-of-the-brain kind of guy with an almost metaphysical approach to creating music. He has developed a "listen, research, think" methodology, which is woven throughout his visceral approach to music as well as his life. "I

Daron Malakian with a vintage Gibson bass, and (below) one of Daron's 40-plus guitars alongside an L.A. Kings hockey stool.

pretty much breathe music," he says. "Everything in my head is music-related."

Daron's home studio space is a reflection of what is going on in his head. His house and studio are saturated with artistic oddities and creative inspirations. The garden and foyer include works of art made by his father (a statue made out of tree stumps) and friends (a tormented skeletal face, made of a rubbery substance, on the vestibule wall). Other areas of Daron's home show that it is a place for rocking out: The kitchen and attached TV room are packed with Old School thrash-metal posters and an amazing collection of guitars (see page 72). A Roland five-piece electronic V-Drum kit sits beside an austere grand piano, and various keyboards and guitars lean against the dining and living room furniture. No corner is left untouched by some kind of musical influence. Daron

A grand piano holds a bust of Mozart plus a few more skulls.

A cadaver sculpted by Bad Acid Trip vocalist Dirk Rogers.

unlocks the door to his "true" studio space to reveal another stratum of musical instruments and art. Guitars, speakers, and amps fill the carpet-lined cavern. A sculpted cadaver with exposed stomach, crafted by Bad Acid Trip vocalist Dirk Rogers, hangs on the back wall. Skeleton heads are situated atop amps to complete the morbid musical landscape. "I am into skeletons and I like skulls. It's a good vibe for me. That's the only way to explain it."

The design of Daron's studio speaks not only to his appreciation for aesthetics but also his spontaneous method of creating. Instruments are strewn everywhere to capture of-the-moment sessions and noodlings. He explains, "It's kind of the way I grew up. My mother and father are both artists, so I was always around art, and someone was always in the process of creating. I kind of emulated that method in my home. The only difference is that here music is the prominent feature, and art is the subtext." Daron continues, "My father was and still is a huge influence on me. He is very focused and driven when it comes to his art, and he creates art because he loves it—not because he's motivated by money. And the money I make doesn't motivate me." The members of System Of A Down have progressed from starving artists to the upper echelons of rock stardom, but Daron sees this only as a stroke of luck to help make a longtime dream come true. "It's strange—I have made some pretty good money, but I don't ever focus on it. I do appreciate that making a bit of money has helped me create this space. I always envisioned having a place where musicians could play whenever or wherever, all day or all night. Now I have that. I really like the idea that people can sit down and play at any time, and musicians can feel free to flow in and out of my house."

"The place where I used to write and create was my room at my parents' house. That was as recent as about two years ago." —Daron Malakian

Indeed they do: Daron's friends flock to his gothic artistic grotto day and night to join in his free-for-all musical jams. Indie rock notables such as Casey Chaos (from the band Amen, now signed to Daron's label, EatUr Music), Zach Hill (from Hella), and the Bad Acid Trip guys (on System vocalist Serj Tanakian's Serjikal Strike Records) find Daron's studio a supreme place to sit and thrash. "At different times, all of us are in there just getting ideas out and jamming," Daron continues. "It's really fun. Many of my friends just like to get together and play."

The free-flowing creative blow-outs often turn into pre-production writing sessions. Daron's converted den helps facilitate capturing the ideas, but the no-frills setup keeps the focus on the music. "I made this den into a studio by having a few guys soundproof the place and then put in a drum set, some instruments, and a PA. Plain and simple." (See gear sidebar, page 72.) This simplicity suits Daron's production style. "For me, simpler is better. It's not a full-on studio where I can take the final product to mastering, but it is a good place for pre-production, where I can listen to and perfect songs."

Fine-tuning tracks for System Of A Down or his own personal use is an uncomplicated, forthright process. Daron's weapon of choice is an Old School boom box circa the

Daron's favorite piece of recording gear: an Old School boom box.

Daron's room as seen from behind the drums.

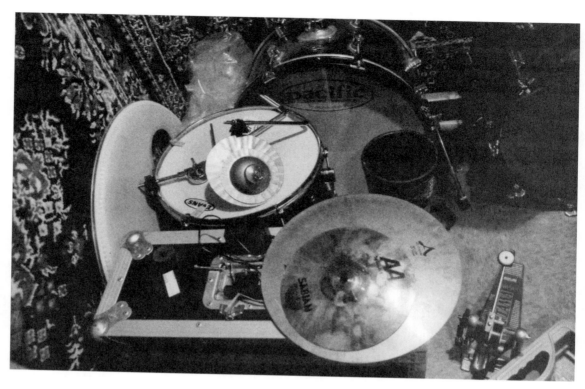

Bits and pieces of the Pacific drum kit.

days of *Breakin' 2: Electric Boogaloo.* "For anything personal, I use the boom box; I've had the same one since I was seven or eight. This box is my personal writing tool—everything I write for myself goes on it. These days, most musicians have moved way past the 4-track to digital, etc., but I haven't moved past the boom box! I'm not even at the 4-track stage. I prefer writing this way."

Documenting songs through a boom box fits well with Daron's "listen, research, think" approach. His favorite tool is not the latest gadget but rather his ear. As a fanatic music collector, Daron has amassed a rich catalog of CDs and LPs that are an essential source of his creativity. "I listen to a lot of records, and I always hear new sounds that I like. I find myself wondering how a band achieved a sound, so I do my research." When something catches his ear, Daron digs into not only the guitars and gear but also the mindset of his influences, and he tries to think as they do. "Whomever I respect, from the Who's Keith Moon to Iggy Pop to Malcolm Young of AC/DC, I try to psychologically get into their same state of mind. I can't say I try to mentally emulate exactly what they are doing or thinking, but I can definitely relate to what they are trying to achieve, and I use that to my best ability when I write and play. I sort of try to capture their creative energy, whether it's in the studio or onstage." By internalizing his influences on all these different levels, Daron can blend them together to create his own distinctive sound. "I might take the snare sound from this album from one era and mix it with a guitar sound from another album from another era, and add my own style. That is pretty much how I approach writing and producing material."

Daron's visceral approach is his strong suit, but he also takes care to keep his technical knowledge up to snuff. "Musicians have to have an ear for music—but they also have to know how to achieve it technically, at least in the sense of understanding a basic mic/guitar chain and knowing how to play around with sound." Eschewing effect pedals and state-of-the-art processors, Daron's guitar crunches are drawn from the guitars and amps themselves—but it's not as simple as it sounds. "It's not about just plugging a guitar into one amp and cranking it. It's about mixing it up with various guitars, different mic placements, and testing out various amps and heads. I basically A/B different setups until it sounds right." (See System Guitar Tuning, page 79.) Always ready to give credit where it's due, Daron adds, "I learned many of these basic concepts from Rick Rubin. I have learned so much production-wise from him; just by listening and watching I pick up so much around him. He has definitely been a big inspiration and a great friend."

In many ways, Daron's home studio space is no different from thousands of garages and converted rec rooms around the country (minus Rick Rubin, the skeletons, and the 40-plus guitars). His setup is straightforward enough for anyone to replicate: Set down some carpets, bring in a bunch of instruments, plug in a guitar or two, and bring in some friends to crank out some music. The quintessential guitarist next door, Daron is a musician who just happened to make it big, playing with a band that didn't quite seem made for the mainstream. "When System Of A Down first started, we thought we could be, at best, a pretty successful indie band. We've just been

A Yamaha PA speaker.

Daron's artistic grotto.

lucky to fall into the right circumstances. I mean, there are a lot of bands out there that people might dig, if they were given the chance." Just remember: Listen, research, think.

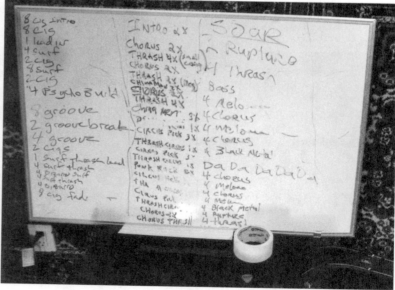

(Left) Ernie Ball strings and a demo tape for Daron's eatURmusic label atop an Ibanez amp; (right) song structures mapped out on Daron's whiteboard.

A mini Marshall practice amp and a Vox T-60 bass amp.

TECH TALK
Collecting Gear

"I don't do much in the way of processing. Instead, I do a lot of A/B'ing of amps, both onstage and in the studio. I mix them around. I complicate things a little by putting various amps and heads together to achieve different sounds. I have 20 or 25 heads and I have about 12 cabs, mostly Marshalls. All of this equipment is not so I can say, 'Hey, look at me—I am a rock star.' It's just that as a musician, it is what I do: collect gear. I am constantly going to music stores looking for new things."

A/B'ing: Testing one piece of gear against another by putting it in the same chain or setup and comparing and contrasting the sounds.

Daron's Soundproofing Tricks

In addition to hiring a few people to soundproof his studio space, Daron improvised and compensated for the room's liveness by placing carpets on the wall, on the floors,

Daron's Guitar Tunings
- Normal guitar tuning—*E* tuning: *EADGBE* (low to high)
- All strings dropped one whole-step (two frets)—drop-*D* tuning: *DGCFAD*
- Lowest string dropped an additional whole-step to *C*—drop *C* tuning: *CGCFAD*

"The System stuff is in a drop tuning: The whole guitar is dropped one whole-step, then the top string is dropped another whole-step—so the whole thing is a drop-*C* tuning. When I write for System, though, I don't necessarily tune my guitar that way. I normally change the tuning when we are ready to play the songs. For instance, I might write a song in *E* for System, but then I'll drop that song to a *C* for us to play it as a band. I like writing things that way. I could drop the tuning all the way to *A*, but I think that sounds a little too typical. I don't like the nu-metal drop-*A* 7-string guitar sound; it is not my thing, at least not yet. Then again, writing songs in *E* tuning also sounds a little too typical to me, so who knows. For me, the drop-*C* tuning is right down the center. It has enough of the clarity and the crisp sound—most of our riffy stuff is done on the top two strings, anyway—but it's also thicker and ballsier."

"I always knew that I loved music—but I never thought I had any real musical talent. For a long time I thought I was just doing something that everyone knew how to do, because it came naturally for me. I guess sometimes you surprise yourself." —Daron Malakian

and over the windows. The result is not only a very cool vibe but also a warmer-sounding room. (Also see No Doubt's soundproofing techniques, page 149.)

Drum Miking Basics

Besides guitar, Daron loves the drums. If he isn't noodling around to create System Of A Down's newest guitar sound, he is playing one of his three drum sets.

Drum miking is a very individual choice. One engineer might use two mics at the opposite side of the room, where another might use 16 mics, five of them on the kick. Below are a few typical drum-miking setups.

Toms: Shure SM57s, Sennheiser MD 421s or 409s, or Audio-Technica ATM 25s, placed two to three inches from the head, pointing slightly toward the head's center.

Hi-hat: Shure SM81, ATM 4041, or Shoepps mic placed close (otherwise the snare bleeds through excessively). It gets very tight in there, so there isn't a lot of room for large mics.

Snare drum: Snares are usually miked at the top head, but it's also common to place a second mic underneath, and switch the second mic's phase. Shure SM57s are a common choice, perhaps with an SM57 or Sony 441 on the bottom.

"Artists who are focused really inspire me. They don't have to be the ones who go wacko onstage; they can be quiet and intense in what they do. I think AC/DC's Malcolm Young ran the show, and he didn't even have to say a word—everyone knew he ran that show." —Daron Malakian

Kick drum: Normally, two mics are used: one for inside the drum and one for the outside. It's best to use dynamic mics for kick drums, as they can take a pounding and handle high SPL (sound-pressure levels). An AKG D-112 or Sennheiser MD 421 is a good choice for the inside, while a Neumann U47 FET is often used as an outside mic. When miking the inside of the drum, engineers sometimes take off the front head and build an isolation area around the mic with duct tape and a packing blanket. An outside mic can be placed near the head or back a foot or so. If you mic farther away from the head, consider draping a blanket over the mic, as the farther away the mic is, the more the snare and additional sounds leak into the kick-drum mic.

Overhead mics: Overheads are normally placed directly above the kit. For this position engineers usually use nice tube mics, such as Neumann 259s.

Room mics: Room mics are generally placed ten to 15 feet in front of the kit. Neumann 259s, Neumann U67s, and AKG C-24s are common choices.

There are some great new drum kits out there. On many kits, rubber isolates each drum from its stand, so the other drums are less affected when you hit one. This makes a difference. Today's drum hardware tends to be very solid, not dinky. Like guitars, drums are usually made of wood, and over the years they can improve—but there are good and bad kits from every era. Some old drums can age well, and some can just fall apart. A Tama Starclassic Performer kit may be able to maintain its sound, while a 1964 Slingerland's sound may fall apart. New drums to check out include those by DW, Gretsch, Pearl, Ludwig, Premier, Yamaha, and Roland.

Chapter Six

The Crystal Method
Glendale, California

"We laugh about the days when we had a sampler with only eight megs of memory."

THE 1962 CUBAN MISSILE CRISIS is rarely referenced within the music community—but the techno/electronica duo of Ken Jordan and Scott Kirkland (collectively known as the Crystal Method) coined their studio "the Bomb Shelter" after a 1960s vestige constructed on their property in Glendale, California. This safe-haven remnant from the Bay of Pigs era doesn't actually serve as the Crystal Method's studio; instead, they created their full-time studio out of the house's garage, naming it after the nearby dugout. But the Bomb Shelter's location is less important than what's inside. Unlike a live rock band's studio, acoustics and room construction are second-

Outside views of the Bomb Shelter.

ary in importance to the computers, software, and gear that form the backbone of the Crystal Method sound.

The Bomb Shelter's makeshift space is strewn with keyboards, compressors, samplers, vintage guitars, and pedals that spill over from the mixing area into the former living room and kitchen. The massive collection of electronics might look overwhelming, but the Shelter marks a stark contrast to the creative spaces where Ken and Scott initially honed their chops: bare-bones bedroom studios in their respective bachelor apartments. Such small spaces and shoestring setups were hardly conducive to the Meth's now-legendary sonic boom. Technological limitations like limited-memory samplers forced the two to spend endless hours creating their subwoofed-out sounds, and the tight quarters meant they had to keep the volume down out of respect to their neighbors.

During these leaner times, Ken and Scott often found themselves debating whether they should hock pieces of gear to buy food, pay rent, or, as Scott puts it,

SHELTER FROM THE NOISE

"One of the great things about having a studio here is that with all of the vegetation in this neighborhood, no one really hears us, so we don't have to worry much about soundproofing," says Scott. *"Of course, having the 210 freeway behind us to mask our sounds doesn't hurt."*

"find a way to keep us above water and hooked up." Now, no longer struggling musicians, the Meth can look back and understand the symbiotic subtleties that paralleled advances in recording technology and the rapid ascent of their recording career.

The Crystal Method's Scott Kirkland at work.

In less than a decade, the Crystal Method saw the Bomb Shelter's gear collection grow from a simple setup to a complex array of tools ranging from analog Minimoogs to virtual instruments; meanwhile, their music transformed from spartan techno beats to more complex arrangements. They have held on to the tricks they learned on older equipment, but they readily embrace present technology—although in small doses, making sure not to overly rely on digital's easy access to canned sounds and beat formulas.

Ken and Scott elaborate on their musical axiom: "All genres of music—whether it is rock, funk, rap, or electronica—are made up of the same fundamentals: rhythms,

One of the Bomb Shelter's many mountains of gear.

An Eventide Ultra Harmonizer, Mark Of The Unicorn 828 interface, and a E-mu sampler.

bass lines, beats, and melodies. If you approach writing and recording knowing that music is made up of variations on the fundamentals, technological advances should not really change your recording perspective. So transforming with technology is simple: We adapt by bringing in what we like about all of the new stuff, but we still keep ourselves grounded in what we used or liked in the past."

The Crystal Method's sound relies heavily on samplers, and Ken and Scott have been continually improving their setup to stay on top of the technology curve. Scott explains, "Throughout our first five years, we combined the stuff we both owned, and we gradually kept upgrading our gear. For our samplers, Ken had an Ensoniq Mirage DPS-16 and an Ensoniq ASR10. I started out with E-mu products; I went from an Emax I to an Emax II. The big jump was to an E-IV." The advanced capabilities of newer boxes like the E-IV provide a marked contrast to the Crystal Method's early days, when Ken and Scott found themselves struggling to find room for their sounds and samples. "We go back and laugh about the days when we had a sampler with only eight megs of memory. Now you can have 256 megs. Our old storage devices were 32-meg or 44-meg cartridges that would fail if the wind was blowing too hard. Now you can buy a drive 200 times bigger, ten times faster, and far more reliable."

To stay up to speed on other hardware, such as compressors, modules, and synthesizers, the Crystal Method would visit Southern California's winter NAMM shows, the annual trade expos where music-gear manufacturers show off their products, from guitars to synths to shakuhachi flutes. Propellerheads at heart, Ken and

One of the Meth's Mackie mixing boards surrounded by a library of music.

Scott would prowl the aisles looking for a low-budget way to keep up on the latest gadgets and gear.

The Crystal Method achieved mainstream popularity with the success of the 1997 album *Vegas* and the commercial airplay of the single "Busy Child." Benefiting from critical accolades as well as crossover appeal, the duo began earning more money—which they naturally spent on new gear. When returning to the Bomb Shelter to record their second major-label release, Ken and Scott were able to take advantage of a wide array of technological advances. Ken explains, "The tools of the trade changed drastically from *Vegas* to the making of *Tweekend*. On *Vegas* we didn't have as many tracks available for digi audio. We had only about seven available voices, so we would use those up right away. The rest would have to be triggered with MIDI through a distortion pedal or something, and then those live things would also be sent straight to DAT." When Ken and Scott sat down to create *Tweekend*,

The Crystal Method's collection of keyboards.

Bass Trap

A bass trap is anything that absorbs low end. If you have a boomy-sounding room, you can absorb some of the low end with large, soft tubes made of soundproofing material. They are most effective when set in the room's corners, where bass frequencies tend to build up.

those technological limitations had become a thing of the past. Better computers with more memory, hard-drive space, and processing speed allowed them to store and create 24 tracks or more at a time, without having to compensate for the gear's limitations. At the same time, they made the jump from 16-bit recording at a 44.1kHz sample rate to 24-bit recording at 96kHz, which allowed them to expand their recordings' dynamic range—from 98dB to 120dB—as well as take full advantage of their drives' higher storage capacity.

These advances affected not only the way they recorded *Tweekend*, but also the way they wrote the songs. Scott explains, "That was a huge part of our development, just being able to have that much more memory and space for recording. It allowed us the time to develop and expand our ideas. But I guess that also became part of the problem." The "problem" was the danger of becoming side-tracked by the new tools and capabilities, or diluting the Method's song-based writing process through endless tweak time. Indeed, *Tweekend* ultimately took over two years to complete, but Ken and Scott still find their new setup much more efficient and conducive to the creative process than the way it used to be.

For *Vegas*, the Crystal Method would often spend up to a month in order to record one song from beginning to end. As part of the process, they spent hours documenting knob settings for each synthesizer, resonance group, and pedal—often in vain.

Several pieces of outboard gear, including an Avalon VT-737 vacuum tube preamp/processor and an Avalon VT-747 stereo tube compressor/EQ.

THE CRYSTAL METHOD ON WIRING

"Our wiring is otherwise known as the Snake Pit," says Scott Kirkland (see photo below). "Instead of messing around with the cables, we just kept it as is—the Snake Pit. If we took the time to rewire, we probably would need only one-tenth of the cables down there."

Scott breaks it down: "With our documenting method, if we tried to bring back an exact sound—whether it was the warmth of a pedal, or its exact levels—there would always be something wrong." Today, Ken and Scott no longer have to record complete songs one at a time; they can store and recall endless variations of loops and

MIDI Basics

MIDI is an acronym for Musical Instrument Digital Interface. A MIDI signal does not carry sound; instead, it specifies which notes are being played, how hard, for how long, etc. Typically, a MIDI signal goes from a controller or keyboard's MIDI OUT jack, through a MIDI cable, to the MIDI IN jack on a device that actually produces a sound of some kind. Most synths and samplers also have a MIDI THRU jack, which allows you to run the same MIDI signal to another synth or sampler—but doing this causes a very slight delay.

song snippets for later sampling and editing. "Having to record one song at a time would really wear us down. At some point you just need to let the song breathe." This new songwriting approach has been a vital part of Ken and Scott's creative process, and it's one of the most rewarding outcomes of their new, non-linear recording style. "Now we can sit with several song ideas developing in a way that we want, leave them when we want, and come back to them when we are ready. It really allows us to work faster and more efficiently, and to be more creative." Scott adds, "It helps us focus on what is a good idea in a song. Good ideas often get lost when you have to worry so much about all the technical details."

With continued success, including numerous placements in film soundtracks and TV commercials, the Method has outgrown the Bomb Shelter—Ken and Scott have decided to pull the plug on the garage shop and move on. But they will always remember the studio's first incarnation with a sense of nostalgia: It's where they grew from an obscure club-culture duo to one of the most recognizable acts in electronica, sur-

An Electrix Mo-FX rackmount signal processor and Peterson Autostrobe R490 tuner.

One of the Bomb Shelter's Mackie mixing boards.

viving the genre's late-'90s trend-of-the-moment status while keeping their clout within the rave scene. "We have been very fortunate to be able to maintain and afford to keep a space where we can work. But there's still something nice about reaching for a knob and hearing a sound change. You can't really replace that."

Ken and Scott are huge advocates of testing gear before using it. Guitar Center, gearhead central for many musicians, is one of the Crystal Method's favorite places to try out gear—mainly due to its return policy. "There have been times when we were just getting into things and we wanted to try out a few pieces of gear, but we didn't want to spend hours at a store with tons of people around us," says Scott. "Guitar Center allows musicians to bring home a new piece of gear to try it out and play around with the gear for a few weeks." Of course, Scott is not advocating abusing Guitar Center's policies. "It's important to do your homework first—know what you are looking for, and how it may help in your recording production."

Making tour plans at the Bomb Shelter.

TECH TALK
Building Old DJ Gear

Scott and Ken explain their back-to-basics approach to building gear with no digital programs, just nuts-and-bolts hardware: "We built a few pieces of gear a while ago. We were touring with this DJ who helped build this momentary-switch-like box. It could be hooked up to a turntable and worked like a gate, so every time he popped the switch, the gate would open and he would get this broken-up sound. We eventually utilized that idea ourselves; Harry Bellord, our live-gear guy, copied the idea and built a similar box. We now take that box out all of the time. Real basic stuff like that—that is what we do. That is about as far as we go."

"We normally just work from our studio. Sometimes we venture into higher-end studios, but I don't see that in the near future, unless we do a mega collaboration with Mariah Carey or something." —Ken Jordan

"We give companies suggestions on how they can make gear a bit better, but they haven't taken them. Beta-testing is kind of a tradeoff—you get to work with something new, but sometimes it doesn't work that well yet." —Ken Jordan

Computers & Memory

As computers and software became more sophisticated, they required more memory in order to run fast enough. Fortunately, at the same time, the equipment was becoming cheaper. In 1994, a 4-meg chip for a Macintosh cost $178; now it costs about $75 for a 512-meg chip. Similarly, hard drives became cheaper—it's now possible to store massive amounts of samples and programs in one hard drive.

Crystal Method Tracking

"Normally we record from the keyboard through an effect pedal," says Jordan. "Then we track into the Mackie board. Sometimes after we are done recording, we send the signal back out to the pedal—but generally it's straight from the keyboard to the pedal." Straightforward tracking methods like these are similar to those used by Devo.

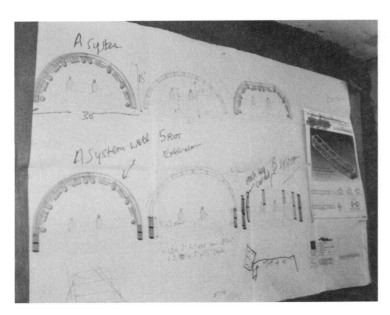

A rough sketch of risers, sound systems, and lighting for a Crystal Method live show.

Favorite Gear

A few of the Crystal Method's favorite synths and samplers include: Nord Lead 2, Nord Lead 3, E-Mu samplers, Alesis Andromeda, and the Roland V-Synth.

Monophonic synth: A synthesizer that can play only one note at a time, not chords.

Polyphonic synth: One that can play many notes simultaneously. The total number of notes a synth can play at one time is called its polyphony.

Analog synth: One that uses voltage-controlled analog modules to create sound. The three main voltage-controlled components in an analog synthesizer are: voltage-controlled oscillator (VCO), voltage-controlled filter (VCF), and voltage-controlled amplifier (VCA). See definitions below.

Resonance group: A panel of knobs on a synthesizer that control resonance. Resonance produces a kind of ringing feedback sound that peaks at certain frequencies.

Sampling: The process of recording a sound into digital memory.

Sequencer: A piece of hardware, or a software program, that remembers things in steps. Digital sequencers use memory to record music on the basis of events (key pressed on, key released, etc.).

Crystal Method Guitar Rock

Despite being rooted in electronica, the Crystal Method is known for its hard rock edge, and Scott and Ken take pride in interspersing rock and metal rhythms and sounds within their music. Case in point: their work with Tom Morello, former guitarist from Rage Against The Machine and currently with Audioslave. "For Tom's guitars we ended up placing his amp half-stack in the kitchen, of all places," says Scott. "It probably wasn't the best place to do it, but that is how we do things around here. We put things where we can find space."

Mastering Electronica Music

"*Tweekend* was mastered by a gentleman named Vladdo—Vladimir Meller—over at Sony," Ken Jordan says. "He has mastered everything from Mariah Carey to Limp Bizkit to Rage Against The Machine; I think *Tweekend* was the first electronic album he mastered. It was kind of difficult with our music, because there are so many different dynamics in there, from bottom to top. We went in with so much bottom end it was kind of difficult, but with his equipment Vladimir was able to capture it. It's important for us to be at each mastering session in case there are questions the mastering technician may have. That way we can answer everything and stay on top of it all."

Console tape for marking mixing-board settings.

Recording & Editing

"When we create a song from scratch we normally start in Digital Performer or Pro Tools," says Scott Kirkland. "We like to record the songs from beginning to end to keep elements of spontaneity within the song structure—something can often get lost when piecing together snippets and samples." Ken Jordan adds, "We normally edit the entire song afterward, after it's complete."

The first time the Crystal Method heard their music on the radio, it was their single "Busy Child." "It was a true test to see if our mixes would sound good. It sounded so wonderful and big on a compressed format, even coming out of a little, cheap, bargain-hotel radio." —Scott Kirkland

Old School Recording/Editing

"In the past we would record and edit through a DAT," says Scott Kirkland. "We would record the bass line and drums on one side of the stereo mix, with the other parts on the other side of the stereo mix. Then we would go in and listen back to what we recorded, we would find little pieces of things that we sampled, and then we'd sample that back into the sampler. At that point we could put two to three minutes of a hard bass line onto the DAT, and then we could gradually slice into it and play along as we edited. We could come up with new forms of that bass line, depending on how we played with it or how we edited it.

"There is a track on *Vegas* called 'Vapor Trail,' where we basically had one synthesizer sound coming out of the Roland SH101. We filtered and manipulated that part to the point where it became several different sounds: the original bass line, a filtered one, a distorted one, etc.—all within the same song, and all created from that one SH101 part.

"The process had its benefits, especially as our samplers began to get larger memory banks. And it made us realize that sometimes the simplest things can be the most creative. Even now we sometimes go back and record and edit through the DAT, but we have sort of cut it out of our regular procedure because we have new tricks."

Roland SH101: A monophonic synth with one oscillator and one envelope. It also has a sub-oscillator (–1 or –2 octaves) that adds depth to bass sounds, making the bass extremely rich.

Digital Performer: A MIDI sequencing/digital recording program made by Mark Of The Unicorn. It is used for editing, arranging, mixing, processing, and mastering multitrack audio projects.

Definitely Old School: a Wollensak reel-to-reel tape machine.

Extra cables and a turntable in the corner of the tracking room—a dance party waiting to happen.

DAT: Digital audio tape, a dedicated PCM digital audio recording format. These days, many engineers no longer use DATs. Most engineers mix to ½" or even 1" analog tape. Even if they record digitally, many engineers still prefer to mix down to tape to get a bit of analog sound into their mixes, even if this adds some tape hiss.

Gear Temperature & Working Conditions

Before the Crystal Method had enough money to buy an air conditioner to properly cool the Bomb Shelter, they often worked in extremely hot conditions. Scott explains, "In the summer, on a typical day here it's around 100 degrees—and with all of our equipment on, it would get pretty warm for us and for the gear. So we had to adjust our working schedule. We would work more toward the evening, leaving our back door open. That would keep things pretty cool." Electronics do not like heat, since it dries out the components, eventually causing them to fail. Therefore, electronics should be

Sequencing central: A Roland V-Synth, a Nord Modular synthesizer, and an E-mu Launch Pad MIDI controller.

Scott and Ken contemplate an Akai sequencer.

kept as cool as possible. Consoles particularly generate a lot of heat, which is why there are often holes around the knobs to let out the heat. As a result the board may feel warm, but it's better that the heat escape.

The Crystal Method's Gear

Hardware and software found in the Bomb Shelter includes: Ableton Live audio and loop sequencer, Akai MPC3000 MIDI production center (sampler/sequencer), Alesis Andromeda A6 polyphonic analog synthesizer, Apple Macintosh G4, Apogee PSX100 AD/DA converter, Arp Odyssey synthesizer, Avalon 747 compressor/equalizer and two Avalon 737 preamp/opto-compressor/sweep equalizers, Avalon Ultra5 Direct preamp, Behringer MX 2642A production mixer, Boss GT-6 guitar signal processor, Bryston power amp, Digidesign Pro Tools, Electrix Mo-FX rackmount signal processor, three E-mu E4 Ultra Digital rack samplers, E-mu Xtreme Lead rackmount synthesizer module, E-mu XL-7 Command Station multitrack sequencer, E-mu Launch Pad MIDI controller, Eventide Ultra Harmonizer signal processor, Joemeek compressor, Korg DTR-1 digital tuner, Korg Kaos Effects Pad, Korg Electribe ER-1 Rhythm Machine, Korg Electribe ER-2 Rhythm Machine, Korg Electribe ES-1 sampler, Korg MS2000 analog modeled synthesizer, Korg Prophecy MOSS-based synthesizer, Korg Mono/Poly analog synthesizer, Mackie Digi 8•Bus 2408 mixer, Moog Memorymoog synthesizer, Moogerfooger ring modulator, Moogerfooger MF-101 lowpass filter, MOTU Digital Performer, Native Instruments Virtual Instruments, Native

Websites

www.vintagesynths.com
www.digitalaudio.com
www.digidesign.com
http://www.motu.com/english/software/dp/body.html (for Digital Performer)
www.native-instruments.com

Instruments Pro 53, Native Instruments Reaktor, Native Instruments Absynth, Native Instruments Ni-Spektral, Native Instruments Battery, Nord Modular Analog Modeling (virtual analog) synthesizer, Nord Lead 2 synthesizer, Nord Lead 3 keyboard, Nord Lead 3 rack module, PC running Sonic Foundry's Acid and Soundforge, Pioneer CDJ-1000 CD-based digital turntable, PMC monitors, Propellerhead Reason, Roland V-Synth V, Roland JP-8000 analog modeling synthesizer, Roland SH-101 monophonic synthesizer, Roland Juno 60 analog polyphonic synthesizer, Roland Jupiter 6 analog polyphonic synthesizer, Roland Juno 106 analog synthesizer with DCOs (digitally controlled oscillators), Roland Jupiter 4 four-voice synthesizer, Shure SM57 mic, Technics 1200s turntable, Wurlitzer Electric Piano, Yamaha CS40M two-voice analog synthesizer, Yamaha CS80 polyphonic analog synthesizer … plus 20 to 30 vintage guitars and effect pedals.

Chapter Seven

Pennywise
Hermosa Beach, California

"Everyone in the music industry—musicians, executives, studios, A&R people—originally got into this business for the love of music. But sometimes that love is lost."

SOUTHERN CALIFORNIA HAS BEEN a punk-rock breeding ground since the late '70s. Prolific bands from Black Flag to the newly restructured Bad Religion have all grown up within and around a stretch of beach from Santa Barbara to San Diego—a region where surfing suburbia's white picket fences make for a rebellious sort that sticks together. It's a community where musicians support each other—where the "no assholes allowed" punk mantra also translates into "no rivalries allowed." The camaraderie that flourishes in the punk community is one of the main reasons longtime friends Fletcher Dragge of Pennywise and Justin Thirsk, former drummer for 98 Mute, combined their technical prowess to create a dynamic two-pronged recording institution. The two collaborated to open up Stall No. 2, a small but state-of-the-art recording studio in Redondo Beach, and Stall No. 3, the rehearsal studio shared by Pennywise and Justin in Justin's Hermosa Beach garage (see Chapter 8). With the assistance of co-owners Byron McMackin (Pennywise's drummer), Mark Theodore (owner of the punk label Theologian Records), and studio engineer Darian Rundall, Stall No. 2 has evolved into an up-and-coming studio that provides an economical alternative for bands seeking professional results at pocketbook-friendly prices.

Justin's backyard garage and Stall No. 2's no-frills setup epitomize the DIY (do-it-yourself) punk ethic; they run counter to the big-studio, big-sell principles that have come to dominate the modern music industry. Now, six years after the studio's initial purchase and construction, the original concept of helping local bands has spread to the music community outside Southern California. Perhaps it is due to Justin and Fletcher's unique friendship as fellow musicians who have experienced the highs and lows of the rock industry. Pennywise and 98 Mute both began as small beach-punk bands, with Pennywise achieving some mainstream success, albeit only after the unexpected 1996 death of bassist (and Justin's brother) Jason Thirsk. This may be an underlying reason why Fletcher and Justin are so adamant about protecting their music-community friends, and why they continue with the notion that creating music can help heal lost souls. To paraphrase Fletcher, it's their own attempt to help bands

Stall No. 2's tropical lounge, complete with bamboo and leopard print.

rise above the self-destructive temptations that often accompany more high-flying, free-spending recording sessions. "To be honest, our initial reasons for purchasing Stall No. 2 were a bit self-serving. We knew that if we owned a studio, we could save ourselves money and use it for our own desires—be the power-mongers ourselves, so to speak—but at some point, that changed. Our love of music in general took over. We knew what bands would encounter within the industry at all levels—from beginning to end—and we wanted to do our best to help."

The demo stage—when bands make rough recordings of a few songs to shop to labels—became the first way in which Fletcher and Justin aimed to help musicians. After seeing several local bands get ripped off during demo transactions, Fletcher and Justin made it a point to take care of novice musicians. Few young bands have a fundamental understanding of what is involved in making studio recordings, or know how to get the type of finished product they want. They often head into a halfway proficient studio with a jaded engineer behind the board, festering and disinterested in any of the demos he has heard this week. Even worse, the engineer may decide to

The Trident 80 C: 32 channels with 24 EQ'd monitor returns. The nearfield monitors are Yamaha NS-10s and Genelec 1031As.

Aloha from Stall No. 2—Wish you were here!

use the band as a tool to promote his own career, selling himself to the bands so he can sell the bands in return. Whatever the situation, the bands are often charged a few thousand dollars for a tape that sounds horrendous but will supposedly guarantee them a listen from top record executives and attain the goal of a major-label deal. Fletcher postulates that studio economics are the root of the problem. "The recording studio is a money-in, money-out business. It's hard to make a profit in general, so some smaller studios charge more to make somewhat of a profit. But we figure, why take it out on bands? We work with a low base rate for the smaller bands; it's actually lower than what we paid when we first recorded here back in 1996. And we'll stick to that rate as long as we can pay our bills." Fletcher and company know that recording an album is a high-risk venture no matter how you do it, so they opt not to charge bands the up-to-triple markup for odd expenses common at major studios. Also, if a band goes over by a bit, they aren't locked into overtime fees—larger

The control room, with Trident mixing board, Neve 8-channel sidecar, and an array of outboard gear including preamps, compressors, and equalizers.

studios often charge double the rate per overtime hour.

Fletcher and Justin's second mission is to battle the music-industry mentality of placing recently inked or A-list established bands into the most expensive studios and tacking on a high-profile producer to nail that No. 1 hit. But the industry's fear of recording at smaller studios is archaic and unjust. Fletcher explains: "It seems like the record companies want to invest a band's money for them—so bands wind up spending $300,000 or more to record a CD. This is ridiculous." He continues, "There is this notion that small studios are good only for overdubs, not for an entire record. There is also the notion that the rooms sound better, just because a famous artist used to record there. Stall No. 2 is inexpensive compared to larger studios, but that doesn't mean our gear or personnel is inferior. At the end of the day, it should be about the band's songs and sound rather than the room or board."

Fletcher's point is especially valid for bands that are recording their first album, or have recorded one album on a label but haven't yet sold enough to secure a spot on the roster. These bands are normally in a do-or-die situation: If they don't score that hit, they will be dropped and left in debt. The label can write off the loss, but the bands have effectively borrowed hundreds of thousands more than necessary to produce the record, ensuring that they will never see financial returns on their efforts. For instance, in 1999 Incubus

Pennywise's Fletcher Dragge and producer/engineer Darian Rundall outside Stall No. 2.

Who says a giraffe can't be punk?

was on the brink of being dropped from Immortal Records after two critically acclaimed but commercially unsuccessful albums. The label's solution was to place them in a top-dollar studio and bring in a big-name producer. Luckily, Incubus wrote several radio-friendly hits, so the label stayed behind the band—but it could have turned out very differently.

Fletcher, having produced several bands (including Justin's 98 Mute), questions the motives of producers who lead bands into studios they cannot afford. "There is an option out there when it comes to recording: an option to pay less. If you're a label, why

Beach life in Southern California.

not put money back into the pockets of your bands, both large and small? Where is the harm in that? The song is what it's about, and sometimes the best things we have ever heard were recorded in people's basements. Look at Sublime's '40 Ounces to Freedom'—that was recorded on an 8-track. It's not about the studio name. It should be about being comfortable where you are in order to write and create and be your best."

Stall No. 2 may have some strategic foresight built in as well. Artists are becoming more and more savvy in their home-recording techniques; the mediocre-sounding songs once generated at home are sounding increasingly professional. The role that larger studios will play in the recording industry in the next few years is already in question. Perhaps only the music industry itself is keeping the high-end studios alive. Whether or not big-budget recording continues to be a mainstay of the pop music business, Fletcher vows to remain steadfast in his mission. "Everyone in the music industry—musicians, executives, stu-

A small gear closet with a fake palm tree and real Fender amp.

dios, A&R people—originally got into this business for the love of music, but sometimes that love is lost. For me, the love of music in all forms is still there. It's fun for me to come into a room with a band, listen to new music, and be a part of that new vibe. Stall No. 2 is more like a hangout than a business for us. We work to continue to create great music. There may come a time when we can turn around and make a profit—but no matter what, we will remember that we are a true musicians' studio, owned and operated by musicians."

TECH TALK
Third Strike & Stall No. 2: A Case In Point

"The band Third Strike came down to record a demo at Stall No. 2, with Darian engineering and producing," says Fletcher. "The band and their manager shopped it around to various labels, and Hollywood Records ended up saying, 'We love this band and want to sign these guys. This demo sounds professionally done. Where did you do this?' They gave them the regular 'money talks' speech, and Third Strike signed with them.

Pennywise Signal Chains

Vocals: Neumann M147 tube mic into vintage Neve preamps, followed by a Neve 33609 compressor, then into the Chandler LTD-1, or sometimes the Avalon 737 EQ. Then it goes to tape or to Pro Tools.

Guitar: One or two Shure SM57 mics and a Sennheiser 421 on a 4x12 cabinet, which go into two Chandler LTD-1 preamp/EQs. (The LTD-1s are based on Neve 1073s but have more EQ frequencies.) The Chandlers' outputs go into a Brent Averill Neve summing box and then to tape or disc. "We usually track guitar and bass in the control room with the amps in there as well, so we can make adjustments on the amp itself for EQ," says Darian Rundall.

Bass: "We always try to use an SVT amp miked with a Shure SM7, an idea I borrowed from engineer/producer Joe Barresi. That goes to a Neve 1272/1073, or the Chandler LTD-1, then to a Neve 33609 compressor. For direct recording I usually use a DI box with a Jensen transformer in it—a homemade piece I bought at a pawnshop—or a Valvetronix tube DI. This goes into the Chandler LTD-1 or Neve 1272 to an 1176 compressor, usually with a 4:1 ratio. Occasionally we use the Avalon 737, but only for EQ."

Compression ratio: A 4:1 compression ratio means that for every 4dB the input goes above a certain threshold level, the output will go up only 1dB. A 4:1 ratio is fairly mild compression. Some units, like 1176s, have several buttons with designated compression ratios, e.g., 4:1, 8:1, or 12:1.

Drums: "All of the drum mics go to the Neve broadcast sidecar except for the overhead mics, which go to Jensen/Hardy Twin Servo mic pre's. From there it goes to tape or disc with no EQ. The kick and snare go into a Focusrite Red 3 compressor, then a Red 2 EQ, another idea from Barresi. The rest of the drums go straight to tape or disc from the Neve."

"Hollywood Records' Third Strike team looked at other high-end studios, like Henson and Westlake, for the recording of the band's debut album. Third Strike's manager knew they could save money by recording at a smaller studio and suggested that Third Strike and Hollywood continue to work with Stall No. 2. He made the point that the demo they loved so much was recorded there, with Darian Rundall engineering. At some point in the conversation, Hollywood must have figured out that if Third Strike did their demo at Stall No. 2, the place must be really cheap—in their minds, a 'price 'em low' kind of studio. Hollywood's people seemed to be under the impression that you can't do a record at a place that caters to the musician and not the record company per se. Third Strike was persistent, and Hollywood finally decided to deviate from the norm, on the condition that they could come down and give Stall No. 2 the white-glove test.

"The producer, Mudrock, came along and gave it the okay, so Hollywood finally gave us the go-ahead. Third Strike made the record here and mixed a few songs here as well. It sounds great. If you put it next to any other record finished in a big 'name' studio, it sounds exactly the same, which dispels the myth that a band must record at a large studio. Why pay $2,000-plus per day to track the guitars in an iso booth just like ours? It's that incestuous show-biz thing, where it's all about a name."

How Stall No. 2 Saves Money

Fletcher explains how his studio keeps operating costs down:

No runners. "We hire runners and interns only for big projects. Small projects must use the 'I buy, you fly' policy."

No stocked fridge. "No refrigerators full of beer, specialty fruit drinks, energy drinks, etc. We supply water and soda—that's it. If you need something special, go out and get it during the break or before the session starts."

Limited gear rental. "We use mainly our own gear. Sometimes we ask our own musician friends in the area if we can borrow a piece of gear. Rentals are only a last resort, except for mics."

No cable TV. Our cable connection was illegal, and the cable company literally cut it off from the pole. So you see we are on a budget here."

No drum doctors. "Stall No. 2 and [Pennywise drummer] Byron McMackin set up a deal with Pork Pie Drums. We have a kit in the studio for any band's use at any time, which is perfect for bands that fly in from the East Coast or from overseas. Instead of renting a kit, we have one ready and waiting for the band, so they don't have to pay an arm and a leg for a drum-tuner guy to come in and order food off the band's label budget."

No catering to artists' studio whims. "Especially for bands who get their first sweet taste of success—no strippers to entertain the kids, and no time is taken out of our day so a guy can get his first introduction to hard drugs."

Purchases over $100 are for studio gear only. "We had a request from a producer's Pro Tools guy. His back hurt; he was used to Aeron chairs and wanted us to buy one. They cost $700 to $1,000, so we told him, sorry, no dice. Instead, I went to Office Depot and bought a knockoff for $100. You can't even tell the difference."

Home-Core Room Tuning

Tuning the control room is essential to obtain mixes that will transfer properly outside the studio. A properly tuned room will allow a mix to sound spot-on from the mix

Pennywise drummer Byron McMackin's Pork Pie drum kit is always set up and ready to go.

Darian's Personal Gear Collection

Neve 33609 stereo compressor
Tube Tech LCA2B stereo compressor
Focusrite Red 2 stereo EQ
Focusrite Red 3 stereo compressor
UREI 1176 compressor
Two Neve 1073 line/mic preamps
Four channels vintage mic pre/EQ from a Quad 8 console (a Quad 8 was used to mix many Motown records; the sound falls between a Neve and an API)
Two Jensen/Hardy twin servo mic pre-amps
Lexicon PCM70 reverb
Two Yamaha SPX90II multieffects
Lexicon Prime Time 93 delay
Roland SDE3000 delay
dbx 160 compressor
dbx 166 stereo compressor
Akai MPC2000 w/SMPTE upgrade
BBE 802 Sonic Maximizer
Dynafex stereo noise reduction unit
Alesis D4 drum trigger module
Forat F16 drum trigger module
Digidesign Digi 001 system
Pro Tools III TDM system

room to the car stereo to the home CD player. In tuning Stall No. 2's control room, acoustical engineer Steve Brandon—a.k.a. "Coco"—found that the control room had a lot of midrange reflections coming off the walls behind the listening position. Basically, sound was being transmitted and reflected all over the room before hitting the ear. Coco advised that the most effective way to minimize this would be to use diffusers to absorb and redirect the interfering reflections over a broad range of frequencies.

"Coco told us pretty much everything we needed to do, and he also advised on building some diffusers," says Fletcher Dragge. "I didn't want to spend tons of money, so he pointed me in the right direction for building my own—from the materials needed to the positioning of each piece. After we finished there was a dramatic improvement. The mixes translate 100 percent better. Now if we burn a few mixes on CD to play in the car, it sounds pretty much like what you are hearing in the room. Problem solved."

DIY diffuser materials: 703 pressed fiberglass or six-pound-density fiberglass, covered in burlap (bought from fabric store and made to fit).

Dimensions: 4' high x 1'7" width nominal (4' x 1'6⅝") x 5¹¹⁄₁₆" deep

Overhauling Stall No. 2

A major studio overhaul was necessary after purchasing Stall No. 2 in 1997. The former owner, professional session drummer Gary Ferguson (Eddie Money, Stevie Nicks), left the studio in a barren and dirty condition, with a small 16-channel Trident

REAL-TIME TRUCK TESTS

A common technique used by producers/engineers is to listen to their mixes in the most authentic atmosphere possible: a car or truck. Fletcher and Darian took the truck tests one step further: They ran cables from the studio to Fletcher's truck in the parking lot so they could instantly hear what the takes sounded like. Fletcher would call Darian on the phone and tell him to turn the kick drum up or down, or add more or less punch to the guitar. But the real-time truck tests ended abruptly when they became too time-consuming to set up.

The gear closet in the back of Stall No. 2.

board and a selection of outboard gear that Fletcher called the "Leaning Tower of Pisa." Today, most of the studio's gear and mics are new; nothing remains except for the 2" tape machine and the Neve Broadcast sidecar.

The old console was replaced with a 1989 32-channel Trident 80 C. According to engineer Darian Rundall, one reason they decided on the Trident 80 C was they could afford it. More important, though, Fletcher really liked the 80 C. "It's a good rock board with lots of punch. It doesn't have a crystalline high end, which is good for the stuff Stall No. 2 does—punk and rock."

"We made sure that no bands were booked, and we allowed ourselves plenty of time," Fletcher continues. "We soon found out that a complete studio overhaul—including carpeting, painting, general cosmetics, and board installation—was not an

The Pro Tools|HD2 system.

overnight adventure." Everything was done on their own time and with their own energy. "Several friends helped us load up the board with a rental truck. It took about seven of us to maneuver it and bring it back to the studio—a major undertaking." As for the actual installation, Pennywise guitar tech Hans Busher wired the board and patch bay. "Hans is great; he goes through all of the components to make sure everything is kosher. If there are caps that need to be replaced, if things need to be rewired, or if something is wrong and he can figure it out, he takes care of it."

The studio's cosmetics took a different route. While boards and gear were being upgraded, Fletcher's look for the studio was slowly taking shape. Aside from carpeting the studio in deep maroon and painting the live room and lounge a bright yellow, Fletcher went for a tropical décor. Bamboo went up in the control room—which actually helped to dampen the high frequencies—and a faux-leopard print went up on the other side of the control room walls. "At first we tried to put felt behind the bamboo, but the sound became too dead, so we took out the felt but kept the bamboo in. I've never seen anyone do that before."

Pro Tools|HD2

All studios must stay competitive. Stall No. 2 is no exception, and to continue to evolve, it must stay in step with the latest in pro-audio technology. Stall No. 2's biggest investment was the new Pro Tools|HD2 (high-definition) system. Like many, Darian Rundall and Fletcher were unsure about digital recording, but both have learned to embrace it. Darian states, "When I was working with Win Davis at Total Access, I was introduced to a Mitsubishi 20-bit 32-track machine with Apogee converters. It sounded great, so I could never say digital was only for the weak." Darian explains how digital made him think of recording in an altogether different manner. "I knew that in order for an engineer to make digital sound as good as analog—or the way the ear is used to hearing analog—there has to be a new way of recording into digital. A lot of anti-digital people are using analog engineering techniques that aren't compatible with digital tools. You have to change something—the mics, setup, gear, how it goes into the board, or the Pro Tools system itself." Fletcher adds, "If you really want things to sound natural, you have to take it live in one take. Also, at Stall No. 2, we feel that moderation is the key to using Pro Tools. Pro Tools is great as far as editing goes—playing around with doubling the chorus, or trying the intro and outro as bookends. But in stuff where every beat and every note is perfect, the sound seems repetitive."

Darian Rundall On The Neve Sound

"I was working with producer Joe Barresi—a complete Neve guy—on Pennywise's *The Land of the Free?* He really got me into old Neve outboard gear. Before working with Joe, I used

A stack of gear including a Tube Tech LCA2B stereo compressor, a Neve 33609 stereo compressor, UREI 1176 compressor, Avalon VT737 mic pre, Manley Pultec limiter/compressor, and Lexicon PCM70 reverb.

Neve 1073s only for drums and the Jensen Twin Servo mic preamps for guitars. That changed when Joe brought his arsenal of Neve gear to Stall No. 2. He made a pure Neve believer out of me. They have punch and power that I never could get on the Jensens. Jensens have great clarity, but the Neves just have a pro rock sound you can't get anywhere else. Now when we track, we have everything we need. If we can't get the sound we want on the board, we can get it through any piece of our outboard gear."

Chapter Eight

98 Mute's Justin Thirsk
Hermosa Beach, California

"We're all getting older, and things have changed."

FROM THE OUTSIDE, Justin Thirsk's garage studio looks like an everyday storage shed—but inside there is a load of gear crammed into a claustrophobically small space. Supplied with fundamental but distinguished recording amenities, including a piece of the Los Angeles Great Western Forum's arena soundboard and part of Pennywise's PA system, Justin's garage studio has become the recording sidecar to Pennywise's Stall No. 2. Rather than start out with a makeshift recording setup and progress to a fully functioning studio, Justin (former drummer for Hermosa Beach's speed-punk band 98 Mute) took the opposite route. "This garage actually came into being as the aftermath of Stall No. 2," says Justin. "We built it about a year after Stall No. 2 was up and running. Basically, 98 Mute wanted a place to play and rehearse close to home. At the same time, Fletcher and Pennywise's original plan to use Stall No. 2 as their own place to record wasn't working out. More and more bands began to book Stall No. 2, and Fletcher and the guys didn't want to pull the power-monger trip—you know, kicking out bands because they own the studio. So our minds meshed, and we came up with this garage studio—now called Stall No. 3."

Stall No. 3's purpose was to be the creative hub for 98 Mute and Pennywise, a place where they could come and go and record as they pleased. 98 Mute and Pennywise made a pact that they would use Stall No. 3 only for their own bands, with the rare exception of a few local friends needing a space, or side projects like Fletcher's the Wheelers. Justin elaborates, "98 Mute and Pennywise have been long-time friends, and it just seemed right to make the pact. Gear could float between our bands, but we didn't want to start getting a bunch of other bands traveling in and out of this small space, because it would have been crunchy. We liked having the space just to go and create without the extra worry."

Only a handful of bands make enough money to live solely off music. Musicians in most smaller bands—98 Mute included—have to hold down 9-to-5 jobs in order to support themselves. It's hard for musicians to keep a full-time job and still take the time off to tour, or even to write and create. Even though 98 Mute has officially disbanded, Stall No. 3 proved beneficial for its members' music careers. Justin continues, "If we didn't have this space, we wouldn't have finished our last album, *After the Fall*. We wouldn't have had the time to make the entire album from scratch—writing, recording, mixing."

By recording makeshift demos, 98 Mute was able to use Stall No. 3 as a virtual workshop where the guys could keep their regular schedules while working separately on music. One or two of them would get together and work out their ideas, making recordings for the others to pick up on and refine. Rough tapes of tracks made the previous night became 98 Mute's main method of communication. Justin explains, "We would leave out tapes for the band members who hadn't heard the new material. They could play them on our garage boom box and then create their parts. We worked efficiently and we were able to maintain our schedules without worrying about how many times we sat down together to write."

The writing process for *After the Fall* was eye-opening for 98 Mute. Justin and the band came to a crossroads that many bands encounter at some point. "We decided we were over the touring. We're all getting older and things have changed." As often happens in bands, their love of music was still there, but time constraints and the music business grind—or some combination thereof—took their toll. 98 Mute didn't want to add new band members, nor did any of the guys want to start a new band from scratch. At first, they decided to stick together and only make records. Justin

98 Mute's Justin Thirsk.

Cerwin Vega and Carvin PA systems.

explains, "We told Epitaph that we didn't want to tour anymore. We explained that we understood if they wanted to drop us, but that we would like to continue working with them if they wanted us only as a record-producing, non-touring band." Since 98 Mute were low-maintenance and never asked the label for tour support or other extravagances, Epitaph agreed to keep them on the roster. "They were cool with us," Justin says. "The only thing they said is that we may not get as many ads. It was the perfect scenario for us at that time." A few months later, though, 98 Mute officially threw in the towel. Justin continues, "We were glad we even had the opportunity to make one album and show it to our friends—but now we have four albums under our belts, and they all seemed to sell around a couple thousand. So the label made money and we didn't. In the end, we just didn't want to put the time and energy into something that wasn't cost-efficient for us."

Justin enjoyed the band's musical journey, but he could have done without some of the other trappings. "I guess I didn't connect with the politics that go hand-in-hand with being in a band: the interviews, the radio play, the magazines that will write a story

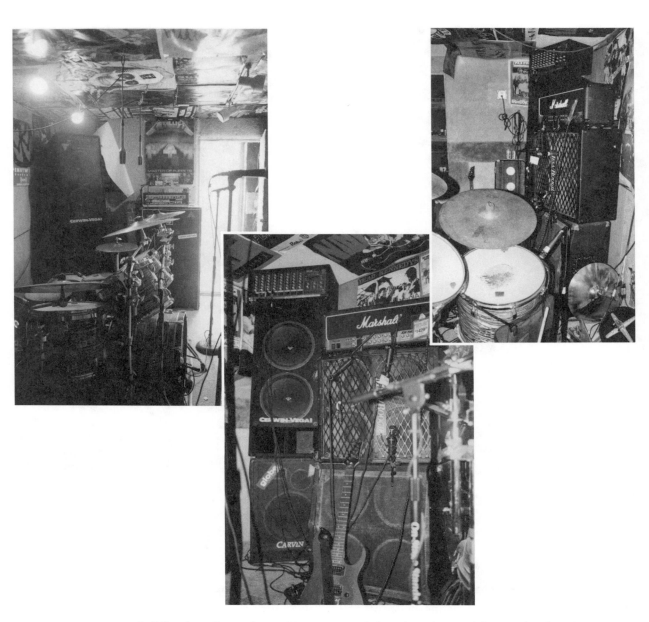

Stall No. 3's small space houses PA systems, Marshall stacks, guitars, and drums. A few Shure SM57s are used as overhead mics and placed against the speaker cabinets.

on you only if you sell enough or if you are cool enough for the 14-year-olds' scene. Things and people change. Right now I just want to write and play as a musician and not worry about these other things that come into play when you are in a band."

Even though Justin and his friends have ditched the 98 Mute moniker, they still get together at their own little recording spot to pound out a song or two, but this time it's for themselves—and Stall No. 3 allows them that freedom. "If we can write music and play together, we are happy. Our backyard garage studio is perfect for that scenario. It lets our creative energy out whether we have a label or not."

TECH TALK

Tracking At Stall No. 3

"Our Teac Tascam 15 Series arena PA mixing console came out of the Los Angeles Great Western Forum," says Justin Thirsk. "Fletcher just picked up that board from a recording equipment auction. It turns out the console was formerly used for the PA system—not concerts—so it is pretty basic, but it's perfect for recording our demos. It is just like any big board, but we don't fiddle with the knobs. You can get some variety on it, but it was constructed mainly for live sound. You turn up or down the snare and toms, you know, and that's it. Play and record—through the board to the Fostex B-16 ½" reel-to-reel tape machine.

"Our board has 16 tracks and 16 inputs. We don't have any compressors or any outboard gear, so our recording technique is pretty rough. But it is fun, and we can actually do a lot on this board, yet in a fairly simple manner. We record drums, guitar, and bass all at the same time. On the drums we use six mics placed in the usual places—toms, overheads, etc. On the guitar we place three mics on one guitar cabinet, but we use only one mic at a time. We don't place a mic on the bass cabinet; we take a direct line from the amp into the board. If we use all of the drum mics, we just record the bass on another day.

"Once we have our initial tracks down, we record overdubs if necessary: back-

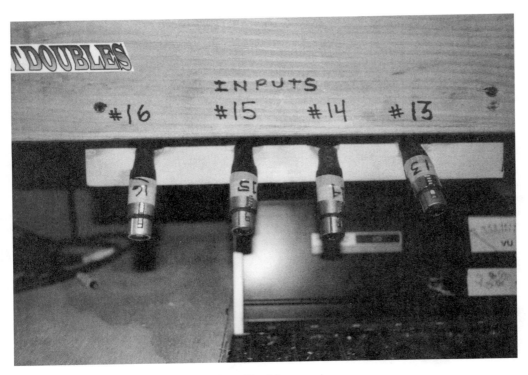

Vocal inputs for the Teac Tascam 15 Series Arena PA mixing console.

Justin's drum kit, fully miked.

ground vocals, additional guitar, etc. When we record the second guitar, we are basically doubling our first guitar's riff; this helps us get a thicker sound as well as have a guitar sound in each channel, both left and right. This is where we use the second mic on the guitar cabinet. We may also do some additional guitar overdubs with the third mic on a different track.

"Behind a door adjacent to the live room is the garage control room, a compact area four feet wide by 12 feet long. We normally use the control room to track vocals.

We devoted four inputs for vocals and background vocals. The singer can go into the room, shut the door, click in a mic, and sing along to the take with the speakers blasting. The music from the take bleeds in a little, but not much—we can handle it."

98 Mute's tracking setup: Six tracks (drums) + three (guitar) + one (bass) + four (vocals) = 14 tracks. Two additional tracks are left open for extra effects.

The Teac Tascam 15 Series arena PA mixing console and Fostex B-16 ¹/₂" reel-to-reel.

How 98 Mute & Pennywise Soundproof A Garage

1. Take the original garage frame's measurements.

2. Staple two layers of carpet to frame.

3. Put up layer of drywall over carpet.

4. Construct another frame of walls and a flat ceiling with wood, following the garage's new interior measurements.

5. Add two more layers of carpet.

6. Add one more layer of drywall.

7. Add one more layer of carpet and soundboard on the roof.

Chapter Nine

Snoop Dogg
Diamond Bar, California

"Top of the line, plain and simple. That's what it is, baby."

WELCOME TO THA CHUUCH, Snoop Dogg's home studio, where Old School spirituality seamlessly blends with Snoop's more licentious side. Gospel music plays in the background, while a few scantily clad women flash on a large-screen TV. It's everything—and yet nothing—that people would expect.

From the outside, Tha Chuuch—one of three homes Snoop owns in the area—has the appearance of any other house on the block, but past the doorstep it's clear that the inside is all Snoop. Several life-size Doberman-pinscher stuffed animals, an

The Doggfather, framed and mounted in the living room of Tha Chuuch.

electric-blue carpet, and a wall-size "Doggfather" poster with a shiny chrome frame are just a few of the ways Snoop marks his territory. Atop a stairwell laced with his countless pictures, Snoop Dogg himself sits behind closed doors at the hub of his creative space.

Snoop has converted the spacious master bedroom into a plush control room complete with a picnic table and several TVs. Towering over the Mackie d8b mixing board with his lanky frame, Snoop gets up for a predictably laconic greeting. In his unmistakable drawl Snoop calls his engineer to work: "Put up some Snoop Dogg music—I need to make some changes." He slips into a soulful vibe, crooning, "When I am alone … would you sex me … I will do anything you want to make you happy." Snoop's mannerisms reflect his well-known pimpish guard, but after he tweaks a few songs, it's evident that underneath his banter lies a hard-boiled and competitive work ethic.

Snoop's no-nonsense approach to his home-studio work began when he relocated his setup from one of his older homes slated for renovation. The former studio was not proving conducive to the creative process. "My previous studio was called the Dogg House, and people treated it like a goddamn doghouse," Snoop explains. "No work got done." Snoop's change of locale gave him the chance to start anew. He makes sure that everyone who sets foot to work in Tha Chuuch respects the grounds. "I want people to come in here the way you would any other church—with a good

The lounge/living room, downstairs from Snoop Dogg's two control and tracking rooms.

attitude and a good spirit. If you come in here with those things, you'll work hard and write and record great music." The trick worked: Everyone who works here does so with a certain sense of spirituality; money is perhaps not the be-all-and-end-all. This in turn helps the musicians stay on top of their game and stay competitive—the key to Snoop's success.

At this stage of his career, Snoop knows most of the traps and games within the music industry. (Witness a couple of his album titles: *Da Game Is to Be Sold, Not to Be Told* and *Paid tha Cost to Be da Bo$$.*) Snoop understands that his role within the rap world's infrastructure is not only as an artist but as a commodity. In the cyclical music business, artists are constantly re-evaluated; if an artist is not selling enough product, he or she often drops from the public eye, soon to be replaced with a new (and perhaps strikingly similar) face. Snoop's determination to stay on top is seen not only in his personality but also in his business philosophy—and in Tha Chuuch's unique setup. Snoop has transformed two bedrooms into separate control rooms. Both rooms have the same boards and same equipment—gear that is, as Snoop puts it, "top of the line, plain and simple"—but each room has a completely separate role. Snoop explains: "The first room was built for side projects or songs and albums that are in the developing stage. It's also a place where artists go to create, write, sing, and what-not." If anything is good enough to make it out of the first room, it can jump to the second room, where Snoop always creates and records. "Anything that makes it to my main room becomes a high priority." This is one tactic Snoop uses to keep everyone

Snoop Dogg at his Mackie d8b board.

he works with in a competitive state of mind. "People can't just come in here; they have to earn it. It is a privilege to work in this bit of Tha Chuuch."

Dave Aron, one of Snoop's engineers since 1993, says there is no question who is the boss here. "Snoop is always expecting the best from everyone and is always keeping mental notes. As long as everyone in Tha Chuuch is doing their thing—writing, recording, etc.—Snoop will never say anything. The tricky part is that Snoop prefers to let people dig their own graves. If they are goofing up, he may not say anything—and if they don't figure it out for themselves, they are gone. He doesn't have to say a word."

Tha Chuuch allows Snoop Dogg to create and take part in all of his various proj-

---

DAVE'S FAVORITE MICS

*"I have a Marshall MXL-V67. I bought it because it was $200, and I think it has a 2"
diaphragm—that's $100 per inch," jokes Dave Aron. "But it does sound good. I also have a
Marshall MXL-603, which is very similar to a Neumann U87; I swear, it works almost as well
as the $1,000 mic. I never have any problems with it. I've only had problems with my HHB
Radius 50 mic preamp; it's great if you don't push the headroom, but if it overloads, it sounds
like crap. The rest of my mics fill out the standard kit: Shure SM57s, Electro-Voice RE 20s,
RE10s, an AKG 451 replica, and a few other workhorses."*

(From left) The entryway to Tha Chuuch; a few posters decorate Snoop's main control room; a framed mug shot of Frank Sinatra—Ol' Blue Eyes is one of Snoop's favorite artists.

ects around the clock, which in turn helps him to continue riding the crest of his status as a rap/pop culture icon. Clearly, Snoop Dogg's work-hard-or-die-hard principles have helped him stay on top of the music industry. "It's the competition. To be in the Top Five and run with the best of them, to still make good music and to still be respected after so many years, to stay and be on top—that is what keeps me going. That is what I strive for."

Tha Chuuch's control room No. 1.

TECH TALK

The Mackie d8b Plus

Snoop fell in love with the Mackie d8b Plus console (Digital 8•Bus with cards). The same studio setup is found within the homes of Snoop's engineer Dave Aron, and colleagues including Fred Wreck, Bootsy Collins, and Soopafly. Aron explains how the Mackie board works within Snoop's camp: "When Snoop got hooked on that little

Up close with the Mackie D8b board.

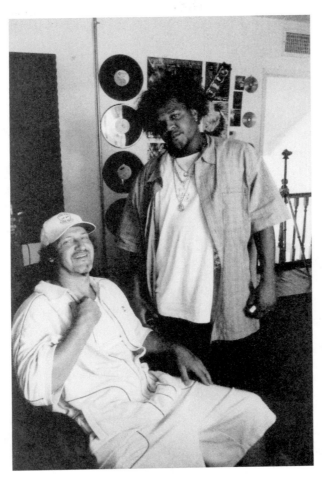

Engineer Dave Aron (seated) with one of Snoop's up-and-coming artists, Sagg.

Mackie setup, he bought a whole bunch of them. Since I was always working at Snoop's studio, I was able to experiment with the Mackie on a daily basis. I began to understand the board's ins and outs. Eventually I realized Snoop and I would be doing a lot of his work on the Mackie, so I thought the best way to really understand the setup was to buy one for myself. I fell in love with the board so much that I gave my previous Soundcraft 400B console to my former Banyan bandmate, Steven Perkins, drummer of Jane's Addiction. I was used to using SSLs all the time, but I found the Mackie was the next-closest thing for the size and money."

Dave reports that the d8b is user-friendly and fairly easy to learn. "Within the board itself are eight good-sounding reverbs, which I use quite a bit, EQs, and effects—you can route them wherever you want. The digital internal patching is what I really like. With just a couple of mouse clicks, you can put a reverb on whatever channels you choose, and you can easily daisy-chain a chorus effect on a vocal and then have it go to a reverb, etc. I use the eight optical ins/outs from Pro Tools Digi 001, plus the eight

View from a Marshall MXL-V67 microphone.

analog ins, for a total of 16 at one time. I like to digitally cross-patch the outputs around for convenience. It has plenty of inputs, so there's room for quite a few returns. I also have three Tascam DA-88s returning on the three banks of TDIF I/Os, and I can switch from the Pro Tools on ADAT optical I/Os to the DA-88s on TDIF I/Os at the touch of a button. And now that Snoop and I have basically the same Mackie/Pro Tools setup, we can transfer material back and forth from his studio to mine almost perfectly. If Snoop wants me to mix a song, I can easily bring it to my home studio, mix it, and come back with it that night or the next day. If we need to make any adjustments, we can load it up and make the changes at his studio, or I can go back home and make the changes there. It creates so many options—I don't have to fight so hard to make things happen as I did on the analog Soundcraft board. It's not that the music comes out better; it just makes working more straightforward and convenient. If the engineering is less arduous, it allows everyone more time to be creative."

Recording Snoop's Vocals

For recording vocals, Dave Aron usually follows this signal chain:

1. Sony 800 mic with a heatsink (basically a big piece of finned metal on the back to keep it from overheating)
2. Avalon 737 preamp
3. Mackie board
4. Vocals bussed to Pro Tools for playback and editing
5. Tracks mixed through the Mackie to Pro Tools' stereo track
6. File exported from Pro Tools
7. File burned to CD using Roxio Toast
8. Song remixed if necessary; otherwise, CD taken to mastering

Mastering is the process in which an engineer sets each song's overall level, equalization, and compression so that they're even with one another on the consumer's final product, the CD. A good mastering engineer examines the variances of each song, one at a time, and makes necessary adjustments.

CD to mastering: Two types of files can be put onto a CD to take to the mastering lab. One is a Sound Designer II file, which is what Pro Tools exports; the other is an AIFF (audio interchange file format) file, like those on audio CDs and read by home CD players. SDII files can be of superior quality—such as 24-bit resolution rather than 16-bit—which is fine for mastering. The mastering lab simply copies the file into its computer and assembles the CD there. Mastering labs can use AIFF files, but the sound quality is inferior: Since CDs are 16-bit at 44.1kHz (just like AIFF files), it is impossible to improve an AIFF file's sound during the mastering process. Therefore, for mastering, it helps to submit song files in the highest-quality format.

Snoop Mixing Techniques

Dave Aron explains the process with which he and Snoop Dogg typically mix songs after tracking is complete:

1. Separate and cross-patch the Mackie inputs. Separating and cross-patching means deciding which faders on the Mackie are going to correspond to which Pro Tools tracks. It's simply organizing everything into a workable palette. For example, track one on Pro Tools (Mackie fader one) may be only kick drum, while faders two and three may be the left and right channels of all of the drums together.

2. Arrange Pro Tools' outputs.

3. Apply sub-grouping and EQ, using the Mackie's compressors and EQ.

4. Balance the sounds' levels as appropriate.

5. Automate the mixing moves. "I use automation only on either the Mackie or Pro Tools—rarely both at once—so I can easily trim the levels on one system after automation is put into the other and the faders' moves are locked."

6. Finish deciding where to mute, etc. "Arrangement is a huge part of the mix."

7. Touch up. "I send the mix off to Snoop, and he decides if changes need to be made."

8. Print mix back to Pro Tools stereo track via S/PDIF.

9. "Once the mixed tracks are back in Pro Tools, I highlight 'export the file' and mix off the Mackie's separated outputs, not from Pro Tools' stereo out or the computer." There are different ways to mix or make final adjustments to a mix. Some engineers prefer to mix entirely

The outboard gear in Snoop Dogg's control room No. 2.

within Pro Tools (commonly known as "bouncing to disk"), while other engineers prefer to send the tracks into the board, mix within the board, and record the mix back to Pro Tools. Dave prefers to combine both approaches: By separating out the tracks and then dropping them back into a Pro Tools stereo track, Dave is basically submixing within Pro Tools, then sending the mix through the Mackie for additional compression and EQ, and finally back to Pro Tools. Dave believes this allows him to achieve "a fuller, deeper sound."

Dave Aron's Ready-To-Go Setup

"Everything in my studio is hooked up and ready to roll," says Dave. "My keyboards come up on one set of faders, all of the DA-88 tape machines come up on another set, and all of the Pro Tools tracks come up on another set. My MPC3000 returns on the same fader groups, and all of my effects come up on the same section I always like to use, or I can re-patch them if I want. The mic is always hooked up to channel 24, ready to go. A snake stays ready to be run for drums. Everything is hooked up the way that is most comfortable and effortless, and if at some point I need to adjust the setup, I can do it easily at any time. That flexibility goes a long way. Previously, if I wanted a delay I could spend hours hooking it up, and sooner or later I would say, 'You know what? I don't want to hook up the delay. I don't need it.' If people are standing there waiting for you, you are often just wasting their time. This system helps my creativity because it works so well for me. I turn up the dial, I push up the fader, and it's a done deal."

Live Snoop Recording

"I have Tascam DA-88s that I kept from the old days," says Dave. "They are great to have. I'll take the DA-88s or Snoop's Tascam 2424 back to the house and mix tracks down, perhaps for a live album. I have recorded almost all of Snoop's live shows with

An Akai MPC3000 used for sequencing and sampling.

this setup, including his tour with the Chili Peppers as well as his tour with Jay–Z and 50 Cent. We even had a Pro Tools studio on the bus for that tour, and we worked on it constantly. We did a big part of *Welcome 2 Tha Chuuch, Vol. 3.* on the bus"

The Tascam DA-88 is an 8-track digital recorder that uses tape. DA-88s can be chained together to record 16, 24, or more tracks. The limitation is that they record at 16-bit resolution; Tascam subsequently came out with the DA-98, which is a 24-bit machine. Sony also made a digital recorder similar to the DA-88 called the PCM-800. Dave normally uses the Tascam 2424 for live recording now. "It records all 24 tracks at once, with no sync lock, and it imports to Pro Tools easily."

Understanding Mixing

Automation simply means the use of a computer to remember all the mixing-board moves made during the mixdown. Fader moves, EQ changes, and panning can all be remembered by the computer, and the moves can be recalled and changed days or weeks later. For example, weeks after a mix is finished, the engineer can do a mix with more vocal while everything else stays exactly the same. Most automation systems are fairly easy to use; it's like having a player piano that you can edit.

Levels refers to the relative balances between a song's sounds. It takes some hands-on work to really understand how level-setting works. The bass level can be changed to match the drums, then the other instruments can be added in perspective,

A Korg T3 synthesizer.

with the vocals brought in so they stand out enough above the music. An engineer can set one instrument's volume and effects to the desired level, then introduce a second instrument, etc.—but in reality, every mixing engineer develops his own method of balancing these levels through experience. Many engineers start with the foundation of the drums and bass, although some prefer to start with vocals. The order of setting the levels doesn't matter as long as the mix's overall picture is the main focus. "I try to determine the main part of the song that I want to feature—vocals, rhythm section, whatever—and start with that," says Dave Aron.

Panning allows you to select where in the stereo field a sound will appear. "You control the left and right like the balance knob on your stereo, but for each sound," says Dave. "You can pan hard-left so the sound plays in the left speaker, or hard-right so the sound is heard in the right speaker only. When you centralize the pan control, the sound is heard equally through both speakers. Changing the panning over time makes the sound travel between the left and right speakers. Certain instruments or groups of sounds are often pushed further to the left or right to make them stand out at different points in the song. Creating a stereo spectrum is a very important part of every mix; every sound in the mix should have its own place. Level controls the depth a sound will have in the mix, but its placement left or right is just as important."

Equalization (EQ) allows the engineer to shape a sound by boosting or cutting certain parts of the frequency range. "I tend to boost frequencies when I'm mixing in

The Hosa Patch Bay.

the studio, and I tend to cut frequencies when I'm mixing a live show," says Dave. "In the studio, sounds are shaped with EQ, and boosting frequencies can bring the sound out front more. When mixing live shows, cutting frequencies is the way to control feedback. There's a balance of shaping the sound and controlling the feedback with EQ."

Filters remove frequencies more drastically than EQ. A filter can prevent unnecessary frequencies from cluttering the mix, thereby cleaning it up overall. There are several kinds of filters. A *highpass* filter is a digital or analog audio device that allows frequencies above a certain frequency to pass through, while frequencies below the cutoff are attenuated. In a *lowpass* filter, frequencies below a certain cutoff point are passed while those above this point are attenuated. In a *bandpass* filter, frequencies around a center frequency are allowed to pass through, while those above and below are attenuated.

Compression: Recorded sounds have levels that vary greatly. At times, instruments' dynamics are not consistent or do not fit the song's overall sound. Engineers use compression to control a sound's dynamic range so it fits better in the mix. Compression also makes a mix's dynamics sound more consistent on different formats (on radio, on CD, etc.) and in different listening situations. A compressor makes it possible for louder moments to be automatically brought down in level while quieter moments are brought up. This affects the sound in different ways. The producer's and engineer's skills come into play here. "If you really crank the compression, the source

Alesis and Yamaha outboard gear.

tends to get very aggressive sounding," Dave notes. "It can work, or it can sound horrible. Proper compression can control your sound and allow you to maximize every sound's overall volume. Compressors are key to putting sounds in your face." Side note: When you're listening to a sporting event either on the radio or on the TV, notice that when the announcer is quiet, the crowd is louder. As soon as the announcer speaks, the crowd goes somewhat to the background. When the announcer is finished speaking, the crowd slowly gets loud again. That is a compressor—with what's called a ducking feature—at work.

A few brands of vintage compressors include: Fairchild, Gates, UREI (1176), and Teletronix (LA2A); newer models include Demeter, Tube Tech, Summit, and Manley. "There are dozens of compressors out there," says Dave. "Have fun just digging into them."

Bussing refers to sending two or more signals to a single output. For instance, if an engineer were using two microphones on an amp, and he had one track available to record on, he could send them to a bus and send that bus to the available track. The channel faders are used to set how loud each mic is relative to the other. The engineer can theoretically add a hundred mics on a bus—everything goes to the one track. (This simple explanation has a million variables.) If you are using only one mic it can be bussed, but it's not necessary.

Monitoring mixes: It is important to listen to every mix to make sure each sound's levels and EQ—or more important, the combined sounds—are correct. It's also imperative to understand the monitoring system's acoustical quirks, so it is crucial to study the characteristics of the monitoring speakers being used in the room you're mixing in. "You must know how the sound will translate to other systems," says Dave. "Custom George Augsperger speakers loaded with TAD drivers are the only soffited monitors I truly trust if I'm mixing at a commercial facility. With a little pair of speakers such as Yamaha NS-10s, you can at least get your mixes' basic sounds and levels. Most studios have NS-10s, but you can also bring whatever you're used to working on. Since you know the NS-10s' characteristics and how they respond to your music, you can get a true picture of what your mix will sound like when it's played somewhere else." It's important to always listen to your mixes in different rooms through different sets of speakers—car speakers, home speaker systems, etc.—to make sure you understand how to compensate for the quirks of your room and monitors. "Most of mixing is eliminating the guesswork and being confident that your mix will translate over to any system. A true monitoring system will do that, so it's the most important tool you have when mixing."

Finalizer: "The T.C. Electronic Finalizer is a piece of equipment you can put the whole mix through," says Dave. "It can EQ, compress, and change levels—all digitally. It's basically a small piece of home mastering equipment. The problem is you can also ruin your mix if you don't know how to use it." Snoop and Dave also use the Finalizer as a digital matrix for monitoring various sources.

Books are written on the mixing process, but it's the actual experience of mixing that makes it real. It's like describing the parts of a car and then trying to drive. A person may know what each piece of the car does, but until they actually step on the gas, they don't know what it's like to drive.

Chapter Ten

No Doubt's Tom Dumont
Long Beach, California

"I never get into editing so much that the original song is unrecognizable."

STONER ROCK, emo, math rock, grindcore, electroclash, garage rock. Genre labels often get tagged on bands whether they like it or not. No Doubt's tag in the early days was Orange County ska. While almost every other band that rode to popularity during "third-wave" ska's moment in the sun has since faded from the limelight, No

No Doubt's Tom Dumont in his ad-hoc drum room. Tom is on a four-piece natural-maple drum set from Orange County Drum & Percussion.

Doubt has maintained its retro ska-wave roots but continues to morph its style without completely transforming the essence of its sound. In doing so No Doubt has been able to accumulate a few more tags—pop, alternative rock, hip-hop, and dancehall, to name a few—and make them all work. No Doubt's strength is a multi-faceted band personality, notably led by vocalist vixen Gwen Stefani. Gwen showcases a strong rocker-chic female persona and the voice of a "real girl" in a pop-music landscape dominated by present and former teen queens who talk like prostitutes. No Doubt is one of the most likeable and versatile bands around—no other label sticks. That's quite a feat for the little ol' band from Orange County that could.

The members of No Doubt have always known how to use a home studio to their benefit, from their early days at Beacon Street (the Orange County house where they gathered to rehearse live material) to the multi-platinum present, when they gather for late-night songwriting sessions in guitarist Tom Dumont's meticulously kept home studio. Tom is the band's self-admitted studio junkie. "I became the little recording guy in the band—I guess because I was kind of good and nobody else really got into it." The layout and purpose of Tom's studio have evolved and grown over time. The space now serves as the launchpad for new No Doubt material, a sonic laboratory for Tom's own ideas, and a production facility for a few local bands and friends. A converted study area now functions as his control room, and a hallway and drum closet provide ad hoc tracking space for Dumont and company.

"We had a little PA system on tour with us, and every night after the show, we would have a little party using this system. We tried to be DJs—we were all terrible."

Tom's project of the moment is the small-in-size but large-in-style multipurpose drum room and closet. The space houses a four-piece natural-maple Orange County Drum & Percussion drum set borrowed from No Doubt drummer Adrian Young, as well as a few miscellaneous pairs of checkered red-and-white Vans and a rack of Old School Ocean Pacific surf shirts. Tom chose the drum room's location due to its proximity to the control room, which allows him to easily run a 16-channel snake cable to his Ramsa board in the adjacent control area. The room's design flies in the face of the careful attention sonic purists usually give to crafting impeccable drum-room acoustics, but this embodies Tom's personal seat-of-the-pants recording style. The "practical" spatial sensibility of the room creates a casual, makeshift vibe that is evident throughout Tom's studio. (Tom has yet to admit whether the clothes rack actually serves a calculated damping function.)

Borrowing from Led Zeppelin's John Bonham, who created astonishing

The 16-channel snake runs outside of the drum area to Tom's control room. A Shure Beta 52 mic resides inside the kick drum.

drum sounds no matter where he set his sticks, Tom tries to work within the room's existing natural tones. Tom explains, "I am not a drummer, but I love to experiment and I love the drums. My general plan for this room is to study up on how they used to mic John Bonham's drums. I just mess around with the placement of about eight mics and see how the sounds change." (See drum miking sidebar, page 145.) Tom's plan emulates the memorable classic-rock story of the recording of *Led Zeppelin IV* (otherwise known as "Zoso" or the "Runes album"): Zeppelin tracked the album in a three-story Victorian house and got unforgettable sounds by capturing the house ambience instead of miking the drums to perfection. (See "When the Levee Breaks," page 146.) Bonham's drumming, as well as Led Zeppelin's natural-sound approach, seem to have made an impression on Tom. "John and Led Zeppelin would get such amazing sounds—sounds that take you back to the basics. That's what I'm aiming for."

"This Ramsa mixing board is the same board we had when we were working out of a little studio in Santa Ana—15 years ago."

The back of the Ramsa WR-TM20 mixing board.

This open-air rock philosophy extends into Tom's control room and his daily routine at the board and behind the computer screen. He maintains that the musicians are the most important part of recording, not the techniques or the tools. The random pieces of outboard gear placed throughout the control room are occasionally used for general experimentation, but he doesn't allow them to distract from the performance itself. Tom's experience recording Gwen's vocals exemplifies his less-is-more theory. "When No Doubt first started out, we would try out all of these crazy, expensive mics for Gwen, saying, 'What mic sounds best for her? What mics make her vocals sound just right?' The mic is important, but I tried to get away from that. When we were recording demos, I would just bring in a decent mic and a decent preamp. Gwen sang and it worked—that's it." (See section on recording Gwen's vocals, page 147.) Tom adds, "If the performance was good enough, we never had to improve the vocal quality with superfluous effects." Most seasoned producers and musicians

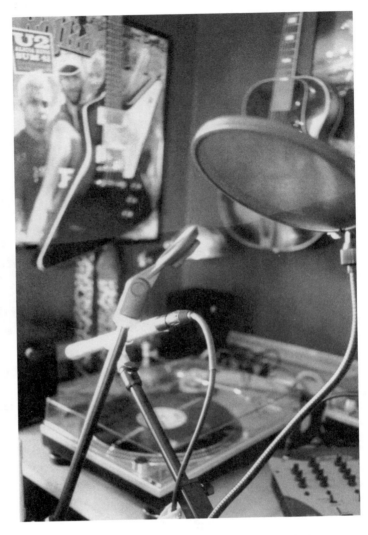

A shock mount and pop filter, frequent home to many vocal mics.

share Tom's perspective is that the performance in a take is of far greater significance than the mic or the equipment being used, but this seems to be less of a foregone conclusion as more and more musicians explore the art of endlessly tweakable digital recording. "In reality, a regular Shure SM57 should work in almost any situation as long as the performance and talent are great."

Keeping the gear simple makes Tom and No Doubt work harder on the songs themselves. "There is something about being very limited that forces you to be more

"I make constant trips to the store, because I am always short a cable or two."

Tom Dumont at his Pro Tools editing station.

creative. It's kind of cool to not have too many options, because otherwise it would bog us down." Keep-it-simple recording was something No Doubt practiced from the very beginning. Many of the quartet's original demos for their self-titled debut and *Tragic Kingdom* came to fruition with just a Fostex 16-track and a few mics. Tom pulls up an early version of "Don't Speak," consisting of Gwen's vocal and a few keyboard tracks. The demo, almost unrecognizable compared to the *Tragic Kingdom* version, worked itself into existence in a basic manner. "We recorded this back in '93 with a few mics, Gwen, a keyboard, the 16-track, and a little Tascam board—no additional effects." Although simple in arrangement, the sounds are recorded to near perfection. As Tom continues to pull numerous tracks off old DATs, it is clear that No Doubt didn't need tons of money to record the tracks well—just great material.

Around the time *Tragic Kingdom* racked up a few No. 1 singles, Tom began to experiment on his PC with Cubase, an entry-level production system similar to Pro Tools. Within a few months he was able to spend one of his first checks on a more expensive Pro Tools system. "Pro Tools was still fairly new and quite expensive at the time, so I was so excited when I got to the point where I could afford it. I couldn't wait to try it out." After working with Pro Tools for the past several years, Tom has grown accustomed to it. "I really know how to use Pro Tools now—at least I feel like it—and I can get what I want out of it. I can use it as a creative tool, or I can use it for editing. It's great for fixing simple problems." Tom demonstrates by pulling up a work in progress. "This super-dub-bass song started off when [No Doubt bassist] Tony Kanal and I were just playing around. We improvised for a few minutes on guitar and bass. It's just like building a house: You put up the frame—in this case we used a click track—and then you add different things to the frame, like keyboard, the bass line, the acoustic guitar with a Fairchild compressor plug-in, etc. It's just fun to use Pro Tools for experimentation".

Tom realizes that it is easy to get carried away in Pro Tools, noting a new twist that Pro Tools puts on production. "In the old days, music was all ears. Musicians were using their sense of hearing to create the music. Now, Pro Tools adds this visual element. Musicians are subconsciously using their sense of sight so they can visualize where things are going. It can be great because it puts this whole other sense in the game—but I guess it can ultimately change how musicians think." Despite his propensity to go into Pro Tools and cut and paste tracks, Tom manages to keep himself in check. "I never go over the line. I never get into editing so much that the original song is unrecognizable." Pro Tools is just an additional element of Tom's basic studio setup, and just another way to record material—in this case, to disk.

As Tom's production skills have improved, he has been able to use his studio and his know-how to make an impact on No Doubt's recording projects and their song-writing process. Tom applied the basic principles he learned from demoing *No Doubt* and *Tragic Kingdom* toward setting down demos for *Return of Saturn* and *Rock Steady*. "We did a lot of the *Rock Steady* demos in my studio—the apartment that I had up in Los Angeles for a bit—as well as here in this space. By just using some basic keyboards like the Trident, Nord Lead, Roland Juno-106, and the E-mu Ultra IV sampler,

(Left) The front of the Ramsa WR-TM20 mixing board. (Right) A Fostex 16-track, the tool of choice for many of No Doubt's early demos.

we were able to get some amazing sounds. We actually used the E-mu's factory samples for a few of the *Rock Steady* tracks, and we were able to get some amazing results on songs like "Hey Baby" and "Detective." By being able to fully develop their songs and sound in an informal environment before setting up shop in a professional studio, the band found that the recording process went smoother, and as a result the songs turned out that much better. "No Doubt was always a live band—that's what we do best by far. We had to learn that there is a huge difference between playing live and being in a studio. It is a completely different spirit, and a process. Having some kind of studio of your own, where you can sit down and play in a recording environment, makes such a difference. Once we started to understand how to record, I think we started to make great records."

Tom and his studio.

Tom explains how writing in his studio helps No Doubt's creative flow: "On *Rock Steady* we recorded all of our material ourselves first; we demoed pretty much all of those songs here. We were creating what we wanted without any outside influences, so we felt free to write whatever. We could write and record a song idea in a day. Just being able to capture that spontaneity—that is the greatest thing about it."

Tom is canny about making music work within his production style, having perfected the approach of spontaneous simplicity. "My studio has been part of a long evolution. It's kind of like being a painter who has been painting for years, but then finally gets all of his canvases and brushes so that he can paint whenever he wants. But the equipment itself doesn't matter after a while. It's just kind of like a stepping stone to get what I want." While technical wizardry and great musical performances

---

"You can make great music with just an 8-track, but you need a certain sensibility. I mean, Shania Twain may not be able to record lo-fi, because it's not really her thing."

---

are far from mutually exclusive, Tom's low-key studio setup and fundamentals-first recording style place the focus on the music—something that bodes well for No Doubt's continued ability to find new, undiscovered variants on their Orange County ska beginnings.

TECH TALK
Drum miking, Tom Dumont style.

1. Set up the drums anywhere you can.

2. Raid your live mic truck or borrow a few mics from bands you know. It's essentially the same thing.

3. Experiment with different mics if possible. They do not have to be expensive.

4. Use little mini Shure SM98 drum mics on the toms.

5. Put a Shure Beta 52 inside the kick drum; this is pretty standard in recording live drums.

6. Place Shure SM57s or 58s on the snare (top and bottom).

7. For more or less all the other mics, use Shure SM58s.

8. Oktava MK012s are used for overheads and hi-hat.

Tracking drums: "I've had these drums for a couple of years, but my drum room is fairly recent. It has been an ongoing project—from getting the snakes to getting my preamp to getting the mics set up and so forth. For now, I basically have eight mics on the drums. I have a 16-channel snake—at some point I may expand and put more mics on the drums—that goes through the hall. I plug the snake into my Grace 808 8-channel mic preamp here; the Grace runs well and sounds great, but it's kind of expensive—around $3,000. From there I have another 16-channel snake that goes into the Pro Tools Mix Plus with two 888/24s. So to put it simply, to record my drums it goes from the Grace to the computer with the Pro Tools setup. I don't record the drums with any EQ, because the drum sound in the room is decent. I've had it set up for only a few months, so I am still experimenting."

EQ on drums: "The amount of EQ depends on many things. If it's a great-sounding drum kit, a great drummer, and a great-sounding room, EQ might not be necessary at all. It is a matter of experimentation. In the end, it's not important how much EQ is used. The sound is all that counts."

Acoustical Acronyms

NC, or noise criteria: An NC level is a standard that describes the relative loudness of a space by examining a range of frequencies; it measures the maximum allowable noise for a given space. NC is important where excessive noise, including background noise, can alter the way sound reacts within a space.

NRC, or noise-reduction coefficient: The average or arithmetic mean of sound-absorption coefficients (which express how efficiently sound is absorbed) taken at 250Hz, 500Hz, and 2,000Hz. The higher the number, the better the material absorbs sound.

STC, or sound transmission class: A numerical rating of how effective a material is in blocking sound. It is a single-number rating of airborne sound transmission that is lost across 16 one-third-octave bands between 125Hz and 4,000Hz. It is normally measured under carefully controlled test conditions. The higher the number, the better the wall or partition blocks the sound.

Tube vs. Solid-State: Some devices have solid-state circuitry, while others have tube. Solid-state designs use transistors and/or integrated circuits; these are usually smaller and require less power to run, so they tend to run cooler. Tube designs use glass vacuum tubes to amplify sound. Tubes have been around for a long time. They are known for their warmer-sounding tones.

Tom Dumont's Gear:

"Blue and white" 450MHz G3 Macintosh computer
Pro Tools Mix Plus w/two 888/24s
Opcode Studio 4 MIDI interface
Glyph dual hot-swap SCSI-drive enclosure
"Lots of temperamental hard drives"
"All the usual plug-ins"
Ramsa WR-TM20 mixing board
Alesis RA-100 power amp
Tannoy monitor speakers
Grace 801 8-channel mic preamp
Daking 522705
Avalon Vt737 mic preamp
API 312 mic pre with EQ
Neumann TLM103 mic
Assorted microphones (AKG D-112, Shure SM57, etc.)
Fostex E16 16-track ½" recorder
Numark Axis 8 CD tweaker

Keyboards

Clavia Nord 3
Clavia Nord Modular
Korg Triton Studio
Korg MS2000 synth
Roland Juno 106 synth
E-mu Esynth Ultra Sampler
Propellerhead Reason software
Korg EM-1 drum machine
Jomox X Base 09 drum machine
Guitars: Assorted guitars by Hamer, Gibson, Fender, Guild, Harmony, Takamine, Lindert
Amplifiers: Matchless Clubman 35; Fender Pro Junior, Bassman 50, and Bandmaster; '50s-era Silvertone combo amp
Drums: Four-piece natural maple drum set by OCDP, cymbals made by Zildjian (borrowed from Adrian Young)
Plus: Assorted effect pedals by MXR, Dunlop, Danelectro, DOD, DigiTech, Line 6, Boss, Naoko Hattori, Matchless, Johnson

The Clavia Nord 3 and Korg MS2000.

How Led Zeppelin Recorded Drums

For *Led Zeppelin IV* ("Zoso"), John Bonham's drums were placed in an open hall or in a small sitting room depending on the situation, while the amps were placed all over the house. Each time they recorded a song, the outcome would be different. The track "When the Levee Breaks" is perhaps the best-known early instance of a huge drum sound using natural ambience and no outboard gear. The setup was simple: The drums were placed in the hall, and on the second landing they placed a stereo pair of Beyer M500s. That was it—just natural reverb. When they needed more kick, Bonham played louder.

Ambient miking works when you have a naturally good-sounding room. Experiment with anything. Producer Nile Rodgers used to cover the entire studio with green trash-bag material to get a great drum sound.

Tom's Ramsa WR-TM20 Console

Tom uses his Ramsa board not only for straightforward mixing, but also as a pseudo–patch bay. Tom explains, "I have the keyboards running through the inputs, but because I work with only one keyboard at a time, I am sending one single signal from the Ramsa to the Pro Tools rig. Basically, I do that so I don't have to keep re-patching them. Right now this board is just a big, stand-in patch bay." Another option is to plug the synth straight into Pro Tools, bypassing the Ramsa's extra electronics to get a cleaner signal—but this can be done only if

Two of Tom's favorite guitars flank a shot of Tom and the Nord Modular by Clavia DMI.

the synthesizer has a line-level output. If it doesn't, the signal has to be amplified through either an outboard mic pre or one in a board.

Recording Gwen Stefani's Vocals

"One of my favorite pieces of outboard gear is the API 312 mic pre with EQ," says Tom Dumont. "I've done a lot of recording with Gwen using the API. We recorded 'Hey Baby' with it, as well as a bunch of other vocals off *Rock Steady*.

"I originally bought this Avalon 737 for Gwen, but I didn't know how to use it right. So I went back to the API. I also recently bought a Daking 52270B mic pre with EQ; the tone is rich and beautiful, and the EQ section is very sensitive. It just sounds rad for vocals. So now the Avalon preamp is kind of obsolete for my purposes."

Mic Preamp Basics

Microphones put out a very small electrical current, so a preamp is necessary to boost the signal to a volt or two—that is enough for a console to work with the signal. The API

Tom's Fender and Bandmaster guitar amps.

One of a few of Tom's guitars hanging on the walls of the control room.

mic preamp is solid-state (using transistors and integrated circuits); the Avalon is tube. Some preamps (like the Millennia Media) have both, enabling the engineer to switch back and forth between solid-state and tube in the search for the right sound. Tom's Avalon also has a built-in EQ, so he can run the output right into Pro Tools without using the console EQ. Of course, if the engineer doesn't need any EQ it's a moot point—but it's handy to be able to EQ the mic signal if necessary. Some boxes now come with a mic pre, an EQ, and even a compressor, all in one unit. It's like having a single console channel in a box. (For more on mics, see Tech Talk in 311 chapter, page 61.) Preamps can be used for anything, really; they just make weak signals stronger.

Tom Dumont's Plexiglass Soundproofing

Tom used plexiglass to soundproof his drum room. Often, by soundproofing a recording room's windows, most of the sound can be contained. A piece of dense material that fits into the window, called a plug, is also helpful in stopping the sound from traveling in and out of the room. Numerous companies can build and fit almost completely soundproof windows (such as the aptly named Soundproof Windows, **www.soundproofwindows.com**).

Soundproofing basics: Soundproofing can be complicated, but in general, soundproof materials prevent sound from coming into or going out of a room. The best way to do this is with *mass*—for instance, lead and heavy materials such as wallboard layers with sand and air sandwiched between them are good insulators.

The sound within a room is governed by two things: (1) the liveness of the surfaces, and (2) its shape. An acoustically solid live room (not the control room) should not have any parallel surfaces at all; no two opposite walls should be parallel. The same goes for the floor and ceiling: The ceiling should be slightly tilted or have many angles. In general, if there are parallel surfaces there will be resonances, as "standing waves" of sound bounce back and forth between the surfaces. That is what you are trying to avoid.

The room's surfaces can be made of very live material such as granite and plaster, or dead material such as shag carpet. Additional devices—moveable panels with wood on one side and fabric on the other, for example—can be used to fine-tune the sound if necessary. It's best to have a range of these surfaces and materials in a room; otherwise the room may be either too live-sounding or have no ambience.

"I often check a mix just by playing the song and walking down the hall. The hall gives me a different perspective. Using a car stereo system is another good way to check mixes."

The Matchless Clubman 35 guitar amp.

Websites for professional sound-proofing materials:

www.auralex.com

www.knoxfoam.com

www.ase.com

In the control room, it is okay to have parallel surfaces. Usually the front window (the window looking into the live room) and the back wall are parallel, but there is enough absorption or deflection on the back wall so it doesn't present a problem.

Soundproofing components:

Mass. An easy (but perhaps not the most technical) way to reduce the amount of noise that travels through walls is to build more mass within or around the walls. The more mass a wall has, the more the wall will stop sound from traveling through. Mass doesn't equal thickness; it refers more to the weight of the material—for instance, a plate of lead can be thin but still have a lot of mass. *Rigid mass* refers to dense mass that is not as pliable; *limp mass* bends sound more easily than rigid mass.

Deadening capabilities. A wall's ability to dampen sound can be enhanced by using layers of material with various masses and densities.

Noise reduction vs. noise absorption: Noise reduction stops sound, meaning no sound is emitted through the wall, window, or door. You can improve this by creating heavier or more dense walls. Noise absorption changes the noise's characteristics through manipulating or managing the noise within the room, usually with different types of deadening materials.

Soundproofing walls: Normally a thicker wall is better—but there are ways to make do with what you have. Air trapped in spaces inside the wall can help reduce noise transmission. Certain types of professional insulation can also help; one kind is Mineral Fiber insulation made by Auralex.

Wallboard (a.k.a. Sheetrock) is the most common way to make walls denser. Add the wallboard layer by layer; normally two layers within a room will suffice. MDF (medium-density fiberboard) and Soundboard (an acoustical product made by Celotex) are also great materials to use.

How to build a wallboard wall: Start with the basic principle of adding on to the walls you already have. Use silicone caulking between the layers; silicone acts as a dampener to help reduce the transfer of vibrations. Apply caulking to the original surface, attach the wallboard with screws, and then use the same procedure to apply the second layer.

Many studios go as far as "floating" the entire room. This means having a room within a room, where the inner room sits on rubber or some other isolating substance, preventing the sound from being transmitted through the floor or walls. This construction method is very expensive.

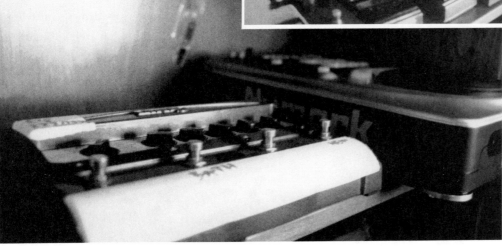

Two views of the pedal closet.

Acoustical Definitions

Dead room: A room containing a large amount of sound-absorbing material, so that it creates very little echo.

Diffraction: The bending or distortion of sound waves caused by a material barrier in the sound field. For example, sound can be heard around a corner because of the diffraction of sound waves.

Diffusion: The random scattering of waves.

Flanking path: The path that sound takes around, instead of through, a partition. Flanking paths include ceilings, pipes, air ducts, doors, and electrical conduits.

Flutter echo: An echo between two parallel, flat surfaces in a room. The resulting reverberation consists of multiple distinct echoes bouncing back and forth.

Frequency: The number of complete sound waves that pass a point at a given time; measured in Hertz (cycles per second). The pitch of a sound is determined by

Transferring Reels Of ¹/₄" Tape To Pro Tools

Tom Dumont has an arsenal of old No Doubt ¹/₄" tapes. He is in the process of transferring them into Pro Tools, so the band's music will be preserved, and so he can store the songs on CDs or DVDs, which can last a hundred years. Tape will easily fall apart by then.

its frequency: The higher the frequency, the higher the pitch, and vice versa.

Live room: A room with very little sound absorption.

Loudness: A term for the subjective magnitude of a sound. A rise of 10dB in sound level corresponds approximately to a doubling of subjective loudness. That is, something that is 85dB sounds twice as loud as a 75dB sound, which is perceived as being twice as loud as a 65dB sound.

Reflection: A change in direction of a sound wave due to a solid object. The sound wave bounces off a surface that is not in the direct path between the source and the listener; it then blends with the direct sound, often causing interference and phase cancellations.

Refraction: The bending of sound waves when they enter a medium, and where the speeds of sound waves are different in each medium. Sound normally spreads in all directions from a point source. Under typical circumstances only the direct sound is received, but refraction can effectively amplify the sound.

Resonance: A characteristic that causes an object to vibrate sympathetically at a specific frequency, or that causes certain frequencies to build up within a room or other space, depending on the acoustical properties of that space.

A keyboard tucked in the corner of Tom's control room.

Keyboards stacked by the control room window.

Reverberation: A smooth blend of echoes in a room. After a sound source stops producing sound, the sound reflects around the room, gradually decreasing in loudness until it is no longer audible.

Reverberation time: The time required for a reverberating sound to decay by 60dB.

Room mode: A "bump" in a room's frequency response, often caused by a standing wave, since the frequency of the bump usually corresponds to the room's resonant frequency. A room mode is determined by the room's dimensions and the fluctuation

of sound energy levels depending upon the frequency, the source position, and the listener's position in the room; and thus the way the sound interacts within the room's space. There are three types of room modes: axial, tangential, and oblique.

Standing wave: A buildup of frequencies between two reflective surfaces, usually parallel with each other. A sound wave traveling in one direction collides with identical sound waves traveling in the opposite direction; the result can be a cancellation or doubling of the signal's loudness at a particular point in space.

Wavelength: The distance a sound travels in the time it takes to complete one cycle. The length of the wave determines the wave's frequency. The wavelength can be calculated by dividing the speed of sound by the frequency.

Chapter Eleven

Korn's Jonathan Davis
Los Angeles, California

"I am a magnet for dark things."

KORN'S TORTURED, dissonant brand of hard rock—extreme vocals strewn within writhing guitar riffs, boisterous bass lines, and rock-hard beats—has proved indomitable, launching the band into what seems like a spontaneous kismet of multi-platinum success. Tenebrous innovators of a musical cult–coined "nu-metal," Korn created a caustic sound that became the soundtrack for a subculture of alienated latchkey kids raised on transparent pop culture instead of adult interaction. These "Children of the Korn" (as Korn's fan club is known) saw vocalist Jonathan Davis as

Jonathan's "jackalope" peers out from the control room wall next to a platinum-record award for Linkin Park's *Hybrid Theory*.

a kind of kindred spirit and found resonance within his maniacally angst-ridden lyrics. Korn's ashen rock image is macabre, abstract, and intense. There's no denying the band's darker side—but this is only part of the mystique within Davis's home studio, a.k.a. Elementree Studios. When talking about the facility, Jonathan exudes a different side of his persona: that of a musician with a focused, inquisitive nature and an obsession with the art of producing music. His home and the adjacent Elementree Studios are a symbol of not only what he has achieved, but also of the passion he has for his work.

Not surprisingly, Jonathan's studio is decorated with all of the trappings of a disturbed rock star. Gargoyles with lasers for eyes leer above the gated driveway, a faux plastic corpse lies above the lounge's large-screen TV, and a "jackalope" head is mounted above the Studer A-800 tape machine. A few of Korn's confidants gather around to see tarantulas clamoring in a cage. Such adornments blend together into a vibrant backdrop for Jonathan's academic intensity: Books are scattered everywhere, from the makeshift kitchen to the tech closet. Jonathan's studio seems tailor-made for his persistent exploration of the unknown.

The allure of music and of recording found Jonathan at an early age. "My dad bought a recording studio in Bakersfield, California, when I was eight or nine years old, so I basically grew up in a studio. It's been a part of me ever since." The music press frequently calls out Jonathan's former career as a mortuary scientist, but despite his morbid public persona, his intentions are often much more endearing than they are disturbing. "For a long time, I actually wanted to be in the studio business with my pops. It's something I've always wanted to do." With the luxury of having equipment like an Otari 24-track and a Trident desk nearby during his formative years, Jonathan got a solid grounding in basic recording principles.

"As a vocalist, Jonathan is the real deal, absolutely. When Korn came out it was hair-band time, but Korn started a whole genre. I mean, no one was doing this stuff before—Jonathan and the boys kind of turned that whole thing on its ear." —Frank Filipetti

"In Jonathan's studio we want to capture the spontaneity and the vibe, and the sound we got while working on Korn's first full album in here is more like the live show than any other record they have done. That is what we were after—something that doesn't sound polished, over-thought, auto-tuned, pro-tuned, and moved. It just sounds like them playing—thank God we were able to capture that." —Frank Filipetti

This also made it hard for Jon to settle for shoestring tactics in Korn's early days. "I hated recording demos on the Fostex 4-track—that was the worst," he remembers. As Korn became a household name, they recorded (and wreaked havoc) in numerous high-end studios around North Hollywood, while Jonathan continued learning more about advanced recording techniques. Driven by the memories of his father's studio—blinded by the knobs, if you will—Jonathan realized that the best way for him to understand the science of recording would be to have his own studio, available for creative outbursts or technical tweaking at any time of the day—or night.

After purchasing a home with a bungalow, Jonathan began to turn his dream of owning a professional level studio into a reality. The bungalow, just a few steps away from the main house, was the perfect place for Jonathan's studio. The bungalow allowed him to keep his home private, but was still close enough so he could write whenever he desired. "I figured I wouldn't have to worry about time. It's in my back-yard, so I can just go out whenever and record when I feel like it." The transformation from bungalow to professional recording facility was a gradual one.

Initially, Jonathan left the structure fundamentally intact and installed a few basic pieces of gear, including a Trident console, a Pro Tools rig, some outboard gear, and a Studer A-800. But this wasn't enough to satisfy Jonathan's growing obsession. "I thought, Screw this—I have this perfect place just sitting there and it's time to go on to bigger and better things. So I went for it. When I finally made up my mind that I really did want to build a full-on recording studio, I knew it had to be different—not of the norm, not just a

Bram Stoker's classic novel *Dracula* and a dragon action figure join the crowd on Elementree Studio's kitchen counter.

A plastic corpse relaxes atop the lounge's large flatscreen TV.

"All the music coming out of here sounds amazing. The thing is, records that are more 'metal' never get recognized. In actuality Korn's sound is much harder to record, without question. It takes a lot more expertise to record." —Frank Filipetti

demoing place for the band." Jonathan developed plans for a full-fledged studio where Korn would be able to record and mix an entire album from front to back.

Perhaps the most challenging part of constructing a new studio is planning proper acoustical dynamics. Knowing this, Jonathan hired prominent architect and acoustician Vincent Van Huff to help with the floor plan. "Vincent is an amazing architect, and I knew he would be perfect for the project. At the outset he blueprinted this huge studio that would have cost me a couple million dollars. I told him, 'That's great and beautiful, but I'm not ready for that yet. I'd like to make do with the bungalow and work from there.'" Even staying within Jonathan's budget, Vincent's new plans outlined what would be an all-consuming project. The endeavor proved to be a test for Jonathan's sanity, but he wouldn't have it any other way. "I am just insane for building my own studio. Even after scaling things down it took a lot of money and time. It may seem a little crazy. I'm just into these kinds of things."

Mic stands and Marshall cabs on the floating concrete floors in
Elementree's live room.

Six months of construction had Jonathan on pins and needles. "The hardest part
was waiting. I wanted to get in there and record from the beginning—really, as soon
as they started construction, I wanted it to be complete so I could get right in there."
Jonathan kept his nerves at bay by staying hands-on throughout the building's renovation. "I think that's why I was here the entire time, being fully involved and watching everything go up. It was an awesome thing to watch." The structure's edifice
appeared almost unchanged, but the rooms inside were completely transformed. The
control room was constructed within the bungalow, while the live room was built out
within the adjacent garage's existing space.

Jonathan expands on the development of the live room: "We walled in the garage
and built stuff on the outside. Basically, we followed the acoustical principles of building a house within a house, or a room within a room." Next, in keeping with the pro-

quality level of their studio renovations, Jonathan and his crew of technical advisers (Vincent, recording engineer Tim Harkins, and Danny Buchanan, Jonathan's personal tech) laid down functional floating concrete floors (see page 162). "We wanted something that allowed for a snappy crack from a drum, so it slams and then pops. We definitely got that. We also got this crazy natural reverberation. We can control that by opening or closing curtains. It doesn't wobble or do any of that shit." Jonathan adds, "I have to say, even though we put a lot of time into constructing the live room, most of the great sounds we get are due to pure luck."

Getting the control room in working order was a bit more calculated—and complicated. Jonathan's board of choice, the SSL 6000, had to be flown in from the U.K. The model is widely available, but this particular board was special for Jonathan. "I love that board because it is solid black. I didn't even know they made black boards until I found that one. I was so lucky and so excited to get it!" The room designated for the board was unusually long and narrow, making it extremely difficult to get the monstrous SSL inside. "When the board arrived, they had ten guys handling it on two dollies. It was too large to bring in, so they decided to take off the legs and run the board in on its side, right through the glass doors." The tight quarters made for other problems, too. The lack of depth in the control room made for suboptimal acoustics for the playback monitors. To tackle the problem, Jonathan managed to hire well-known acoustical consultant George Augsperger. Jonathan explains, "He created these customized main speakers. They're like giant freestanding near-field monitors. They sound amazing!"

After installing the board and mains, a few additional acoustical quirks needed to be fixed. "Vincent came in and looked at the place, took a few shots of the room, and came back with plans to help with the acoustics. He showed me where and why I needed to put the baffles and carpets and everything. Some of the stuff was pretty basic, like adding soundboard and curtains. So Danny, Jim [Monti, Jonathan's assistant and engineer], and I went up on ladders with screw guns. The big speaker stands and all of the baffles—we made that stuff ourselves." Frank Filipetti, Korn's engineer and sonic mentor, added a subwoofer under the control board and damping on the back wall to compensate for diffusion in the control room and the mixing area. (See section on reverberant control rooms, page 165.) With all the fine tuning complete, Jonathan's room is now completely up to professional sonic standards. Frank agrees: "We are getting amazing mixes out of Elementree. The tracks that I've recorded and mixed in there are just as good as—if not much better than—the mixes I have done at any pro studio."

The problems Jonathan encountered building Elementree are on a grander scale than most musicians will ever see, but the persistence and focus he has demonstrated is a big advantage when heading into any home-studio project. In the end, the time Jonathan and his consultants put into Elementree made for an impressive sound—but Jonathan also admits that some of it was by chance. "Sometimes, acoustics can be 100

Jonathan's control room: (left to right) Brian "Head" Welch, Jonathan Davis (standing), engineer Frank Filipetti at the SSL 6000, and James "Munky" Shaffer (seated with guitar).

percent luck. I mean, you could try to build the perfect room, but you'll never know what you are going to come out with."

Building Elementree Studios was a big project for almost everyone involved, but Jonathan's quixotic nature kept him totally committed to the project—and devoted to learning more about the craft. "I've learned a lot with this studio. Before I started to build this place, I really didn't know how to engineer. Having put all of this time into the studio, I absorbed little things—adjusting sound, acoustics, and general engineering techniques. And Frank has taught me so much. He helped me look for gear and recommended I try different compressors like the UREI 1176 and the Teletronix LA2A, the Neve 1073 mic preamp, Tube Tech compressors, multi-band compressors, and the dbx 160 compressor. For digital recording and editing, he helped me learn about the Euphonix R-1 and Steinberg's Nuendo. I've kind of put my Pro Tools to rest, and now I'm diving into those applications." Jonathan sounds more than ready to start working behind the board, but he remains adamant that he's not an engineer, and that Frank and Tim Harkins are the ones who make everything work. "Frank and Tim know the tech side inside and out. I just know what I want sound-wise—scoring, writing, all of that stuff—so I basically concentrate on sound and creating."

At first, people had trouble believing that the bungalow could become a real studio. "I kept telling them, 'It is a fucking real studio, and it sounds amazing!'" Jonathan elaborates on his proudest moment: "Being able to record our entire album

Take a Look in the Mirror at Elementree in only six weeks, and have it sound so amazing—that made me so happy." Jonathan has seemingly satiated his studio obsession for the time being. "I am extremely grateful that I'm in the position to create this style of studio. This is now the home of Korn—everything that is Korn is going to come out of here."

TECH TALK
Frank Filipetti

A Grammy–Award-winning engineer who has worked with an array of artists including James Taylor, Rod Stewart, Hole, and Carly Simon, Frank Filipetti has been Korn's technical advis-

One of Elementree's custom Augsperger monitors.

er and engineer the past few years. Frank gives some insight on the construction of Jonathan Davis's Elementree studio.

Constructing a floating concrete floor: "Floating floors break up the transmission of sounds. By isolating different parts of the studio from each other, you lessen their influence. For example, you don't want low-frequency energy traveling from the bass drum in the studio along the floor into the control room, so you isolate each section by floating the floors on neoprene, or some other acoustically isolating substance."

"I gave the old Trident board to Munky. He has it in his little studio now, so it's still in the family." —Jonathan Davis

---

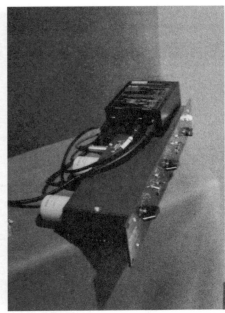

(Left) A computer monitor at the far end of the control room; (right) outboard gear waiting to find a connection.

Fixing low-end frequencies in the control room: "It's very important that at the mix position I hear as clearly and as accurately as I can, but Jonathan's control room has a less-than-ideal shape for monitoring. It resembles a remote truck in that it is very narrow, and there isn't enough depth behind the console for the lowest waveforms to develop properly. Low-frequency energy has much longer waveforms than high-frequency energy. It's just simple physics: Sound travels through air at roughly one foot per millisecond, so the wavelength of a 100Hz tone, which takes ten milliseconds per cycle, is approximately ten feet. A 50Hz wave repeats every 20 feet! Depending on the room's reverberant characteristics, that can create some nasty standing waves. Having room behind the engineer gives the bass frequencies a chance to develop and gives a place for the engineer to do some trapping if need be. Since Jonathan's control room is only seven feet long from front to back, there isn't any room for that. From 150Hz on up the room sounds terrific—but below that, especially in the 60Hz-to-80Hz range, things get a little inconsistent. This is exacerbated by Korn having two 7-string guitars and a 5-string bass, all tuned down a 4th—so there's a massive amount of energy in the lower octaves." To help

Jonathan's Favorite Mic

"I try to figure out what mic is best for me by trying out a lot of them. I've tried a lot of the Audio-Technica mics, lots of vintage mics—but one of my favorites is this amazing Telefunken 251. Besides looking cool, it sounds amazing! They are rare and very expensive. They run from about ten grand to 25 grand. It is awesome, though, because my mic has the number 666 on the side. I swear, weird shit finds me. I am a magnet for dark things."

The Telefunken 251 is a bit of a legend. It was originally sold for around $300. The 251 is a tube condenser mic with a pattern switch that has three settings: cardioid, figure-8, and omni. (See mic section in Chapter Four, page 61.) The ones with an "E" on them were for export to the U.S.; they use a different tube inside. The European versions used an AC 701 tube, and are more desirable.

Telefunken history:
  www.telefunken.com

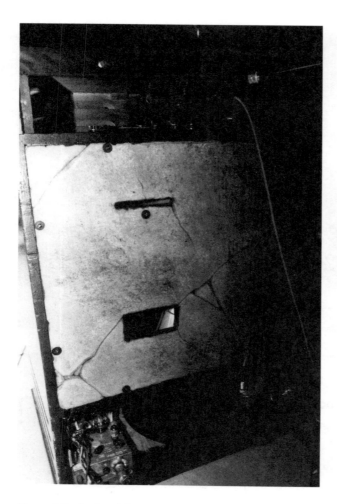

Views of the back and front (with Audio-Technica mic) of a Leslie rotating-speaker cabinet ready for recording in the live room.

Jonathan's Gear Basics

Mains: Custom Augsperger Monitors
Near-fields: Yamaha NS-10s; Genelec
S30Ds with a Genelec 1094 sub-
woofer
Compressors: Teletronix LA2A and
LA3A, two UREI 1176 line compres-
sors, Tube Tech SMC2B, dbx 160
Effects/processing: Eventide H300s
Harmonizer/signal processor, Yamaha
SPX90, AMS-DMX 1580s and AMS-
RMX 16, and various pedals
Mic pre's: Eight Neve 1073s

solve this, Frank got in touch with Peter Chaiken at JBL speakers. "Peter mentioned that JBL was developing a new speaker line that allowed for low-frequency tailoring to room acoustics, so I thought I would try it. Using the JBLs, we were able to significantly smooth out the frequency anomalies." Frank also put a subwoofer underneath the console to get a better feel for the low end. Low frequencies are less directional than highs (it is harder to tell where low-frequency sounds are coming from), so precise placement of a subwoofer is less important than with a speaker that generates mids and highs.

Overly reverberant control rooms: "In about 90 percent of L.A. recording studios, the control room is overly reverberant. All of these studios have wood plenums right where the speakers are, and they have another piece of wood above the speakers pointing right at the engineer. To me, that is the worst thing you can do. It creates short reflections of the direct signal. Delayed reflections are fine to a point; anything above about 80 milliseconds is okay. But a five- or ten-millisecond delay is horrible—all it does is comb-filter the sound. Jonathan's studio had this problem to a certain extent, so I decided to deaden the room. I put up a lot of little fabric pieces with fiberglass or sonics behind the console. I also put up some curtains to deaden the area as much as possible, and we did special treatments to a few really weird spots. Now, with those adjustments, Elementree is as good as any professional studio."

On Recording Vocals

"The main thing is to know the singer's voice," says Frank. "Learn what it sounds like and what makes it different. Some points to consider: What is the voice's frequency range? Where are the harmonics grating? Where are the spots in the voice that may need a little help? Where are the things that add the harmonic content that make the voice distinctive? Look for ways to enhance areas that have unique harmonic content. Boost the frequency bands where the voice might not be as strong, and smooth out the areas where it may get a little harsh. Also, know what each microphone sounds like so it

A cubbyhole houses most of Jonathan's mics.

can enhance the voice; experiment with each and find out. Mix and match in your mind: Say, 'Well, with this voice a Neumann U47 would be a good start.' Then build from there. All of these things went through my mind when I first recorded Jonathan's voice.

"Because of Jonathan's dynamic range and the fact that he can fry a preamp as quick as anybody, I have to be careful in what mic and preamp I choose to use on his vocals. The Neumann U47 has a rising high end and a nice bottom end that enhances his vocals. Jonathan, unlike a lot of rock singers, doesn't really get harsh. Some singers have a 3k hardness that you have to watch out for, but Jonathan doesn't—so the U47 was a good place to start. I also tried a Telefunken 251 and a Sanken CU44. The Sanken is a unique design in that it is a dual-capsule condenser mic. There is a large condenser capsule for the low end and a thinner, quicker capsule for the high end. The built-in crossover is smooth and works well with Jonathan. On *Untouchables* we used a Neumann M49, which worked very well with his voice. We also used a Tube Tech mic pre and a Neve 1081 for EQ; we got a slight bit of compression with an 1176 and a final touch of 'air' with a Massenburg EQ.

"Generally there is a range of mics that will work well with a singer. It's a question of matching the voice's sonic characteristics with the sonic characteristics of the mic, and going from there."

The Neumann U47 power supply, which provides the voltage needed for the mic's tube. The U47's rising high end and large bottom make it one of the best mics for Jonathan's vocal range.

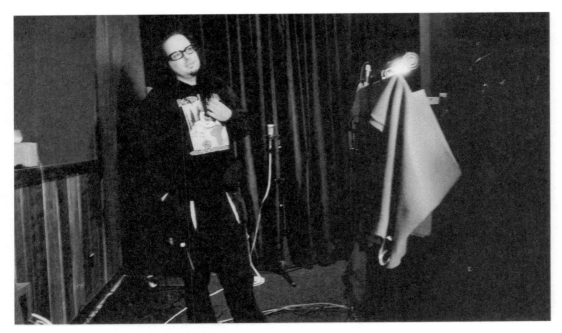

Jonathan describing the dynamics of Elementree's live room.

Jonathan's Homemade Vocal Booth

"The frequency range of Jonathan's voice is from about 250Hz to about 5kHz," says Filipetti, "and in mixes he is competing against guitars and drums, whose frequencies also fall around that range. So basically, all of these instruments are hitting in the same frequency. In order to get the most impact from Jonathan's vocals, I tend to screen off the room reflections as much as I can. We don't have any iso rooms, so we built a foam booth. It's like a three-sided house, with a back and two sides that flare out slightly. We also put on a foam roof." Frank's goal is to record Jonathan's voice very dry, with almost no room sound. "Jonathan's recording space is acoustically very live, which is great for many things—but in this case it would just tend to muddy up the vocals." Room sound can always be added after a dry vocal track is complete.

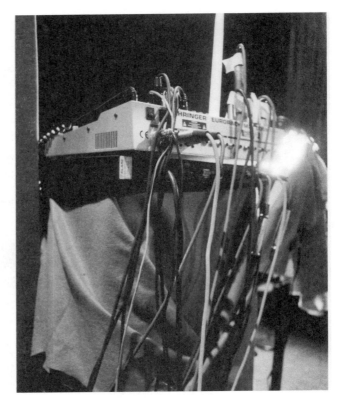

Jonathan's personal cue mixer rests within reach of his homemade vocal booth.

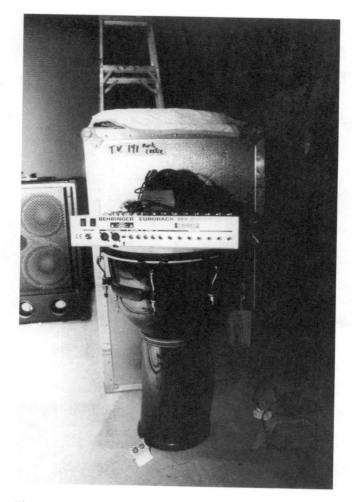

Hi-tech, lo-tech: A Behringer Eurorack MX2004A mixer sits atop a hand drum.

On Recording David Silveria's Drums

When recording drums, the top two things that Frank tackles are phase relationships and room reflections. Frank likes to take on the problem of phase relationships by using the "rule of threes": He likes to use ambient mics to get a big drum sound, but he keeps each drum's direct mic at least three times closer to the drum head than any ambient mic. This helps prevent tracks from being out of phase—i.e., canceling each other out. Frank also has a lot of hands-on experience with the reflections in Jon's room: "It's a very live room, but I was amazed at how well we were able to control it. When someone plays the drums in there, it doesn't sound overly 'roomy.' I was able to get a nice, punchy direct sound on the snare and the bass drum. I wanted to make sure to bring out Dave's tom-toms along with the bass drum and the snare. The major element to control is the cymbals. Boy, when they start crashing, that stuff tends to get

Munky and Head's effect pedals.

everywhere and can just destroy a drum sound. So that is the main issue for me—controlling the metal."

Miking a kick drum with a speaker: One way to record drums is to use a large speaker. Place it in front of the kick drum and use it as a microphone—electrically, a speaker and a mic are basically the same thing. Then add it in to the regular mic mix. By doing this, you can get some really deep tones.

Recording Munky & Head's Guitars

"Head [Brian Welch] and Munky [James Shaffer] play down-tuned 7-string guitars," says Frank. "When recording both guitars—and on top of that, Fieldy [Reginald Arvizu] is playing bass—things can get muddy incredibly fast. So we try to make the guitars sound as direct as possible, where we still capture the amp's power but without a lot of the room sound. To achieve this

A Pro Tools rack and ADAT recorders squeezed in back of the engineer's sweet spot.

(Left) An amp-equipped Fernandes Nomad guitar amid more-sophisticated gear; (right) DVDs and a silver-finished guitar flank Jonathan's favorite xylophone.

sound while recording *Take a Look in the Mirror*, we surrounded the amps with screens. I had three amps on the guitars, but each amp was placed in its own separate homemade foamcore booth. To make each guitar sound stand out even more, Tim Harkins suggested that we not only place foam on the amps' sides, but also put foamcore over the top and underneath each amp. That dimmed the sound nicely and made the guitars clear and punchy."

Guitar mics: Shure SM57s and Neumann U67s. Frank also uses an AT4047 on Munky's and Head's cabinets and adds either a Royer ribbon mic, a 57, or a U67.

Foamcore: Thick foam can be used to isolate amps from each other, and from the room. Frank basically built a little house of foam (about 12 inches thick) to put around each amp.

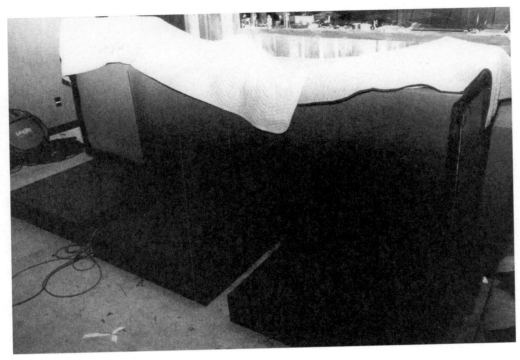

Homemade isolation booths. Several inches of foamcore surround the guitar cabinets to keep the sound clear and punchy.

Recording Fieldy's Bass

"Fieldy doesn't sound like any other bass player," says Frank. "It's important to him and all of the other Korn members that his uniqueness be captured. To do that, I basically listened to what he sounds like playing live, and I emulate that sound on tape or disk." Frank normally lets Fieldy's bass sit above and below the guitar and uses three or four mics on his bass amp.

Bass mics: Frank uses a Sanken CU44X and an AT4047 on one speaker and an AKG D-36 on the other. To capture the high end of Fieldy's tweeter, Frank uses a Shure SM57.

Acknowledgments

Artist Consultant— Lisa Roy

Technical Advisor— Larold Rebhun

A VERY SPECIAL THANKS to all of the artists and people who helped make this book possible:

Fletcher Dragge and Pennywise, Justin Thirsk and 98 Mute, Darian Rundall, Tom Dumont and No Doubt, Jim Guerinot, Paris Montoya and all at Rebel Waltz Inc., Jonathan Davis and Korn, Frank Filipetti, Jim Monti and all at The Firm, Daron Malakian and System Of A Down, Heidi Ellen Robinson Fitzgerald, Rick Rubin, Lindsay Chase, Velvet Hammer Management, Lee Ranaldo and Sonic Youth, Aaron Mullan, Michele Fleischli and all at G.A.S. Entertainment, Snoop Dogg, Dave Aron, BT, The Crystal Method, Josh Sanderson, Megan West and all at 3 Artist Management, Krista Pope, 311, Adam and Peter Raspler at Raspler Management, Michael Beinhorn, Ellis Sorkin, Susan Celia Swan, Matt Griffin, Csaba Petocz, Erin Haley, Bill Ryan, Erik Stein, Kit Rebhun, and my Family.

About the Author

MEGAN PERRY is an accomplished writer, photographer, and insider on the Los Angeles music studio scene. Her work has been published in leading music publications including *Rolling Stone, Alternative Press, Guitar Player, Revolver, Bass Player,* and *Pollstar.* Her monthly "In The Studio" column in *Alternative Press* and work at NRG Recording Studios and Moir/Marie Management gave her front-row access to the recording of many of the greatest albums in recent memory.

Index

EQ IS RECORDING

The newest addition to EQ's roster of monthly features is THE ART OF RECORDING

Everyone knows that in studios today, it seems to be all about computers, DAWs, and plug-ins. But that doesn't mean that producers, musicians, and engineers don't need to know "traditional" recording techniques and how to use hardware.

EQ IS FOR THE PROS

Each month, *EQ*'s exclusive new Art of Recording section features hands-on guides to mic technique, hardware processing, interfacing hardware with software, acoustics, how to get the best performance from an artist, and **much, much more**.

83% of EQ readers are recording professionals, and 75% of EQ's readers own a professional recording studio?*

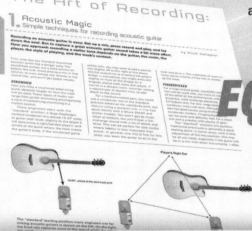

51% of *EQ* readers are full-time recording/music production professionals, and another 32% are part-time professionals

30% of *EQ* readers own a commercial recording studio and 45% own a professional project studio?*

*Information taken from EQ 2003 Subscriber Study

Subscribe now at **www.eqmag.com** *or call 888-266-5826*

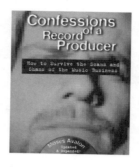